PONDERING(S) TOO

Unless otherwise noted all Scripture quotations are taken from the New American Standard Bible ® (NASB), Copyright © 1960, 1962, 1963, 1968, 1971, 1972, 1973, 1975, 1977, 1995 by The Lockman Foundation. Used by permission. www.Lockman.org

Scripture quotations marked (ESV) are from the ESV® Bible (The Holy Bible, English Standard Version®), copyright © 2001 by Crossway, a publishing ministry of Good News Publishers. Used by permission. All rights reserved.

Scripture quotations marked (MSG) taken from THE MESSAGE. Copyright © by Eugene H. Peterson 1993, 1994, 1995, 1996, 2000, 2001, 2002. Used by permission of NavPress. All rights reserved. Represented by Tyndale House Publishers, Inc.

Scripture quotations marked (Phillips) are from The New Testament in Modern English by J.B Phillips copyright © 1960, 1972 J. B. Phillips. Administered by The Archbishops' Council of the Church of England. Used by Permission.

Scripture quotations marked (CEV) are from the Contemporary English Version, copyright © 1991, 1992, 1995 by American Bible Society. Used by Permission.

Scripture quotations marked (LEB) are from the Lexham English Bible. Copyright 2012 Logos Bible Software. Lexham is a registered trademark of Logos Bible Software.

Scripture quotations marked (MEV) are taken from the Modern English Version. Copyright © 2014 by Military Bible Association. Used by permission. All rights reserved.

Scripture quotations marked (NIV) are taken from THE HOLY BIBLE, NEW INTERNATIONAL VERSION®, NIV® Copyright © 1973, 1978, 1984, 2011 by Biblica, Inc.™ Used by permission. All rights reserved worldwide.

Scripture quotations marked (KJV) taken from the King James Version of the Bible, public domain.

All references to (Strong's) refer to Strong's Exhaustive Concordance of the Bible, public domain.

Pondering(s) Too
Copyright © 2019
Wayne Berry

Cover concept and design by David Warren.

All rights reserved. No part of this book may be reproduced, stored in a retrieval system, or transmitted in any form or by any means—electronic, mechanical, photocopy, recording or otherwise—without the prior written permission of the publisher. The only exception is brief quotations for review purposes.

Published by WordCrafts Press
Cody, Wyoming 82414
www.wordcrafts.net

PONDERING(S) TOO

Thoughts on:

Kingdom Citizenship • Ministry of Reconciliation

Ambassadors for Christ • Channels of Grace

WAYNE BERRY

WordCrafts

KINGDOM LIFE

Spirit come and take control, touch me deep down in my soul
Fill me till I overflow, with kingdom life

Speak to me and I'll obey, every word I hear You say
Lead me in Your righteous way to kingdom life

I long to be like You, in everything I say and do
But I can't live that life, without your presence deep inside

Father, Son, and Holy Ghost, grant me what I'm needing most
The spirit of the Pentecost for kingdom life

(W. Berry / See & Say Songs, BMI)

Author's Note

This is not a book of opinions as such. You already have your own. You don't need mine. Rather, it's a collection of thoughts on subjects that I personally think are worth thinking about—core values of a sort. The intent of the content is to stir you to consider some certain things from another point of view than the one(s) you currently have. If reading it prompts you to think, then I've done my job. My goal is to make the data available for private and public pondering.

"As a man thinketh in his heart, so is he..."
~Pro. 23:7 - KJV

Contents

PREFACE 1
    HURRY UP AND WAIT 7
    A PRACTICING PROVOCATEUR 8

INTRODUCTION 12
    AN ABRIDGED TESTIMONIAL 12
    HIGHWAY OF HOLINESS 17
    KINGDOM LIVING (Thoughts on Worship) 24
    PURPOSED PROSE 33
    DOING THE MATH (An Analogy) 34

CHAPTER ONE: KINGDOM CITIZENSHIP 37
    PROTOCOL AND PRACTICE 37
    A CONTEXTUALIZED APPLICATION 42
    KINGDOM TRANSFORMATION 45
    STUDENTS OF THE WORD 51
    WORDS ON THE WORD 53
    NATIONALIZED CHRISTIANITY 56
    WHO'S IN CHARGE HERE? 64
    THE DOWNSIDE OF DOUBLE-MINDEDNESS 72

CHAPTER TWO: MINISTERS OF RECONCILIATION 78
    TIME MANAGEMENT 78
    RELATIONAL UNITY 80
    RELATIONAL DISCONNECT 85
    RECONCILIATION (On Purpose) 88
    CHRIST'S FAMILY DNA 95

CHAPTER THREE: AMBASSADORS FOR CHRIST 98
SEEING WHAT WE'RE SAYING 98
10 ESSENTIAL QUALITIES OF AN EFFECTIVE AMBASSADOR FOR CHRIST
   [By: Candace Waggoner] 103
HOW TO CONDUCT OURSELVES AS AMBASSADORS FOR CHRIST
A Real Ambassador/A Cultural Representative/Gracious Speech/Common Ground
   [By: David F. Maas]: 105

CHAPTER FOUR: CHANNELS OF GRACE 120
FAITH IN MOTION 126
HOPE AS AN ENERGIZER 128
SOURCING HOPE 131
THE DYNAMICS OF THE CYCLE OF HOPE 134
OUR PLACE IN THE PIPELINE 139
APPROPRIATING GRACE (Apostolically Speaking) 144

EPILOGUE 149

PREFACE

First things first.

From Old Testament Scriptures, according to *Strong's Concordance,* to *ponder* means to roll flat, i.e. to prepare (a road); also to revolve, i.e. to weigh (mentally). And to balance, i.e. measure out (by weight or dimension); to arrange, equalize, through the idea of levelling (to estimate, test).

In the New Testament it means to combine, i.e. (in speaking), to converse, consult, dispute (mentally), to consider, (by implication), to aid (personally). To join, confer, encounter, help, make, meet with.

In *Webster's New Collegiate Dictionary* it means: To weigh in the mind (to appraise), To deliberate about, To review mentally (to think about); To think or consider quietly, soberly, and deeply.

{I am a practitioner of pondering}

Another aspect of pondering is to consider through thought. So, consider this:

> *"You shall love the Lord your God with all your heart, and with all your soul, and* with all your mind, *and with all your strength."*
>
> ~Mark 12:30 (Emphasis mine)

There are four components or characteristics mentioned in Mark 12:30. By and large, the body of Christ tends to sanction/embrace three of them fairly well, while allowing the forth to seemingly survive on life-support. Heart, soul, and strength (the "I can do all things" dynamic of Phil. 4:13), are given a level of importance in our teaching and preaching that rarely balances out with that of the mind.

> *"I've never lived with balance, but I've always liked the notion…"*
>
> ~B. Cockburn

It's as if our intelligence has become a step-child at best in regard to growing up and maturing as believers. How and why we continue to allow that to take place is disappointing (tragic perhaps). It is most certainly not how Scriptures address our minds and how we are to use them. Here are several examples of what the Word says:

> *"Therefore I urge you, brethren, by the mercies of God, to present your bodies a living and holy sacrifice, acceptable to God, which is your spiritual service of worship. And do not be conformed to this world,* but be transformed by the renewing of your mind, *so that you may prove what the will of God is, that which is good and acceptable and perfect."*
>
> ~Rom. 12:1, 2 (Emphasis mine)

PREFACE

"Study to shew thyself approved unto God, a workman that needeth not to be ashamed, rightly dividing the word of truth."
~2 Tim.2:15 - KJV

"Therefore if you have been raised up with Christ, keep seeking the things above, where Christ is, seated at the right hand of God. Set your mind on the things above, not on the things that are on earth. For you have died and your life is hidden with Christ in God."
~Col. 3:1-3 (Emphasis mine)

"Serving the Lord with all humility of mind..."
~Acts 20:19 - KJV

"And as he *reasoned about righteousness and self-control and the coming judgment..."
~Acts 24:25 - ESV

*Reasoned: From a root word meaning to relate in words (usually of systematic or set discourse).

"...I will put My laws into their minds..."
~Heb. 8:10

"The fear of the Lord is the beginning of wisdom, and the knowledge of the Holy One is understanding."
~Pro. 9:10

An Axiom
Knowledge is Information

Understanding is Interpretation
Wisdom is Application

"Place your hand on your forehead and say—'Engage.'"
~Bishop Tudor Bismark

Here's a beautifully stated prayer of pondering, and repentance for restoration:

Abandoning Ourselves to the Goodness and Grace of Our Father

"Whom have I in heaven but you? And earth has nothing I desire besides you. My flesh and my heart may fail, but God is the strength of my heart and my portion forever."
~Psalm 73:25-26 - NIV

"Heavenly Father, as we ponder the impassioned declaration of the Psalmist, we also cry out, "Us too, Lord, us too!" May we live by the mathematics of mercy—faith calculating your unparalleled worth in a world of fool's gold and temporal pleasures.

"Grant us the perspective of eternity, that we might live our days with heaven's hope and its matchless joys in view. Keep us gospel-sane—thinking with the mind of Christ, reasoning by the riches of grace, and worshipping you in Spirit and truth.

"Father, give us more satisfaction in yourself than in any story, situation, or circumstance we might choose for ourselves. Thank you for giving us many gifts to enjoy, but we want you to be the most gratifying feast of hearts—our portion and passion, our treasure and inheritance. By your Holy Spirit, make it so. Make it more true and real to us than ever before.

"Forgive us for our ingratitude and envy, our fears and lack of trust. Free us from every expression of entitlement and demandingness. Heal our gospel-amnesia, Father. We too easily forget that we are your children of delight; your daughters and sons of grace; those you've hidden in Christ, sealed for eternity, and rejoice over with singing.

"Oh, blessed, loving, and merciful Father, we worship and adore you today, and forever. So very Amen we pray, in Jesus' exalted and glorious name."

~Pastor Scotty Smith

Over the last four decades or thereabouts, as a teacher in the body of Christ, I've noticed a common trait among those who've attended my classes and in congregations in general. It is this: The longer people are out of a classroom environment (study, assignments, homework, tests, etc.), the more likely they are to become less active in the ongoing process of learning. The lack of discipline which comes from not being in an educational environment tends to cause people to turn their minds off and coast mentally.

The very act of acquiring and applying knowledge becomes too much of an effort. As a result, people seem prone to relying on data that they've already stored in their heads over time, which they continue to draw upon as they age. The practice of acquiring knowledge, assessing it with understanding, and then applying wisdom no longer fits into their lifestyles. As a result, many (perhaps most folks) rely on what they already know, instead of continuing to be renewed in their thinking.

You can also view pondering through the lens of contemplation. To *contemplate* (from *Webster's*) means: 1. To view or consider with continued attention, 2. To have a view as contingent or probable or as an end or intention; to ponder or meditate. *Contemplation* means: 1a. Consideration on spiritual things as a form of private devotion, 1b: A state of mystical awareness of God's being, 2. An act of considering with attention (to study), 3. The act of regarding steadily, 4. Intention, expectation.

A person who practices contemplation is known as a *contemplative*—meaning marked by or given to contemplation; of or relating to a religious order devoted to prayer and penance. I am such a person.

The Bible speaks of mediation as well. So, to mediate, or to practice mediation is a Scripturally sound method of accomplishing the same goal(s) presented in the terms I've just defined. For example:

Isaac did so in Gen. 24:63. Joshua did so in Jos. 1:8. David did so in Ps. 1:2; 63:6; 77:12, 119:15, 23, 48, 78, 148; 143:5. Paul directs Timothy to do so in 1 Tim. 4:15.

David's meditations continued in Ps. 5:1; 19:4; 49:3;104:34; 119:97, 99.

As I see it, biblically speaking, that places me in good company.

The handling, examining, and unpacking of the things related to living a kingdom life is therefore well worth dealing with. However, in these digital daze we live in, such practices have seemingly become a lost art. To attempt to do such pondering requires far too much time than many people care to bother with. Be advised, what I mean is that there is no app for that.

Such mind-set recalibrating cannot be personally

incorporated quickly. That would in and of itself be a contradiction in terms. Mulling things over mentally most often calls for taking time. And, far too many of us have little to no time available for such activities.

HURRY UP AND WAIT

> *"Step out of the traffic! Take a long, loving look at me, your High God, above politics, above everything."*
> ~Ps. 46:10 - MSG

The Biblical directive of waiting on the Lord encourages us to find the space and sensibility to incorporate such practices as I've just mentioned into our lives. But, often it seems that we don't/won't allow time for that to happen. We are simply too busy, to distracted, or too undisciplined. Without a willing spirit and an obedient desire to wait on the Lord, the pro-active participation of setting our minds on things above becomes an impossible task to try and tackle. I'll have more to say about thought life later. (See Col. 3:1-3)

> *"Don't you know anything? Haven't you been listening? God doesn't come and go. God lasts. He's Creator of all you can see or imagine. He doesn't get tired out, doesn't pause to catch his breath. And he knows everything, inside and out. He energizes those who get tired, gives fresh strength to dropouts. For even young people tire and drop out, young folk in their prime stumble and fall. But those who wait upon God get fresh strength. They spread their wings and soar like eagles. They run and don't get tired, they walk and don't lag behind."*
> ~Is. 40: 28-31 (Emphasis mine) - MSG

A PRACTICING PROVOCATEUR

"And let us consider one another to provoke unto love and to good works."
~Heb. 10:24 - KJV

It seems to me that our understanding of what it means to be provoked tends to be biased in a negative direction. That's too bad. And it's also an incorrect understanding. The results of being provoked can have either a positive or negative effect, depending on the whys and hows of its usage. In other words, *provoke* is what it is, based on its intended use. Perhaps defining the language will help to clarify what I'm saying:

Provoke: *To call forth; to stir up purposely; to provide the needed stimulus for; to rouse one into doing or feeling or to produce by so rousing a person.*
Provocative: *Serving or tending to provoke, excite, or stimulate.*
Provocation: *The act of provoking; something that provokes, arouses, or stimulates.*
Provocateur: *An agent of provocation.*

Another usage of the concept of being provoked is found in Acts 17:16, where Paul says that his spirit was "stirred" within him. *Stirred* (in the KJV) is defined in *Strong's Concordance* as being *sharpened alongside*. It's from the same root word as *provoke* used in Heb. 10:24 which says, *"and let us consider (provoke) how to stimulate one another to love and good deeds."*
Both terms share the sense of incitement (to good) or dispute (in anger). Either definition is appropriate depending on the intention (context) in which it has been purposed.

PREFACE

From that perspective, the idea of *"iron sharpens iron"* interrelates to the idea of provocation:

"As iron sharpens iron, so one man sharpens another."
~Pro. 27:17

Having said that, perhaps it's time for me to just go ahead and come right out and say this: *I am a provocateur.*

I have been for pretty much most of my life. The following story will likely make that clear.

Some 35 years ago, my father died. During the second day of visitation at the funeral home, an event took place which impacted me profoundly. I would have never in a million years expected such a thing to transpire. I'll share it with you here because it has a bearing on what's to follow in this manuscript.

My mother and I were standing in front of my father's coffin receiving condolences from family and friends—both old and new. In the process of doing that, there were people in line that I had not seen in years—some in decades. One of those who had come to show his respects was the pastor from the church that I grew up in—the fellowship where I was "born again." As I turned away from speaking to someone, brother Miles was standing directly in front of me. I couldn't recall the last time I'd seen (or spoken) to him, but it had been long, long ago. He spoke kindness to mom and me regarding dad's passing. Then, he said this (paraphrased as I recall it).

"Wayne, I was always glad that you grew up attending our church. You had such an impact on the Sunday School teachers over the years."

At that point, I was stunned. What could he mean with such a statement? My recollections of those days was that my cousin

Rex and I were always getting into trouble by disturbing the classes. On more than one occasion we were sent out of class to stand in the hall until we could control ourselves (attitude, actions, and our disruptive behavior). That being the case, why would he make such a comment?

I gathered myself together enough to ask him exactly what he meant. Then he said this in response: "You always challenged the teachers to work harder on their lessons by asking them such hard questions."

That is provocation in action.

Picture a scene from a movie where an impactive moment is taking place. The person involved sees themselves as being transported back in time—as if they were in a tunnel traveling backwards at a high rate of speed.

The moment he spoke those words, that's exactly what happened to me! I felt like I was being rocketed backwards over some 30 years or so, into my teens. At that instant it was as if my life came into focus in a way I'd never seen with such clarity. My childhood pastor had just given me a great gift, coming at one of the most emotionally difficult and meaningful times I'd ever encountered.

His evaluation of me (from my childhood through my teen years) was that my way of thinking had been an asset to the adults who were teaching me and my peers in classes, during the very days that I thought I'd only been a problem for everyone in attendance.

When that took place, the Holy Ghost spoke to me saying something to this effect: *"That's who you are, and that's how you were fashioned.*

"For You formed my inward parts; You wove me in my

PREFACE

mother's womb I will give thanks to You, for I am fearfully and wonderfully made; Wonderful are Your works, and my soul knows it very well."

~Ps. 139:13, 14

"...for in Him we live and move and exist..."

~Acts 17:28a

Having shared all that, here's a provocative statement for your consideration: I believe that God's kingdom is *The Context* (#1 priority) for every single aspect of living as a follower of Christ. I'm going to do my best to try and explain why I said that with this manuscript.

INTRODUCTION

AN ABRIDGED TESTIMONIAL

"Let the redeemed of the Lord say so…"

~Ps. 107:2a

I was born in Tennessee, and reared in a typical Southern Baptist Church, with its basic fundamental theology and narrowly-focused sensibilities. However, I am deeply appreciative of what I received in that narrowed and limited spiritual environment. The basics are always important. They are, if you will, fundamental.

I was saved and baptized into the body of Christ there at age nine. My life was eternally changed by what I experienced sittin' in those old wooden pews. At thirteen, I received a "call" of some sort related to service for the Lord, but I didn't understand what that meant at the time. Then at fifteen or thereabouts, I began to drift away from fellowship due to two specific cultural events which were taking place in and around me.

INTRODUCTION

1. My interest in and giftings for making music were expanding way beyond the limits of what was available (or acceptable) in the "house of God."
2. The Civil Rights Movement was exposing the difference between what many Christians said they believed (according to the Bible), and what they were expressing by their actions, attitudes, practices, and proclamations (both privately and corporately).

Both of those factors were pulling me away from congregational life, and into a life lived outside the walls of the church. As a result I became a prodigal son.

STRAY

I've been out on the border, down along the shore
Up over America so many times before
I've been stayin' out of trouble, by stayin' on the street
I've been in and out of luck so many times I'm incomplete

Now it's all I can do to keep away from you
It's been harder than anything I've ever tried to do
I know what will be will be what it will
But I can't keep movin' if my hearts standin' still

CHORUS:

You're a stray just like me, it's written all over your face
You're a stray just like me, you're just tryin' to find your place
Back in 1967 you were L.A. bound
You read in the newspapers 'bout that new underground

PONDERING(S) TOO

You were young and impressionable, and misunderstood
And searchin' for salvation, but it didn't do no good

Now its all I can do to keep my distance from you
Its been harder than anything I've ever had to do
I know what will be will be all it can
But I can't keep movin' if you're holdin' my hand

REPEAT CHORUS:

BRIDGE:

Ain't no heroes left, except the ones on parole
The last call for heroes was light years ago
Like some sleeping Messiah at the side of the road
We wait for directions and then
We'll be briefed on how all this will end
Looks like we've got to go through it, again and again

Just meet me somewhere in America, in the middle of the night
There's a place we can go, where it's absolutely right
All the young visionaries simply dance till they drop
There ain't no need for changin', if that changed, then they'd stop

Now it's all I can do to keep my hands off of you
It's harder than anything I've ever been through
I know what will be in control
But I can't keep movin' if love takes hold

REPEAT CHORUS:

(W. Berry / See & Say Songs, BMI / Circa 1978)

INTRODUCTION

That's an autobiographical narrative. This old hymn says it better.

COME THOU FOUNT OF EVERY BLESSING

Come Thou fount of every blessing
Tune my heart to sing Thy grace
Streams of mercy never ceasing
Call for songs of loudest praise
Teach me some melodious sonnet
Sung by flaming tongues above
Praise the mount I'm fixed upon it
Mount of thy redeeming love

Here I raise my Ebenezer
Hither by thy help I come
And I hope by thy good pleasure
Safely to arrive at home
Jesus sought me when a stranger
Wandering from the fold of God
He, to rescue me from danger
Interposed His precious blood

O to grace how great a debtor
Daily I'm constrained to be!
Let thy goodness like a fetter,
bind my wandering heart to thee
Prone to wander Lord I feel it,
prone to leave the God I love
Here's my heart, O take and seal it,
seal it for thy courts above

Lyrics by Robert Robinson, 1757 (Emphasis mine)

At that point, the sanctifying work of the Spirit picked up where He'd left off.

From: Quiet Talks On Prayer

"A great sorrow has come into the heart of God. Let it be told only in hushed voice—one of His worlds is a prodigal! Hush your voice yet more—ours is that prodigal world. Let your voice soften down still more—we have consented to the prodigal part of the story. But, in softest tones yet, He has won some of us back with His strong tender love. And now let the voice ring out with great gladness—we won ones may be the pathway back to God for the others. That is His earnest desire. That should be our dominant ambition. For that purpose He has endowed us with peculiar power.

"There is one inlet of power in the life—anybody's life—any kind of power: just one inlet—the Holy Spirit. He is power. He is in every one who opens his door to God. He eagerly enters every open door. He comes in by our invitation and consent. His presence within is the vital thing.

"But with many of us while He is in, He is not in control: in as guest; not as host. That is to say He is hindered in His natural movements; tied up, so that He cannot do what He would. And so we are not conscious or only partially conscious of His presence. And others are still less so. But to yield to His mastery, to cultivate His friendship, to give Him full swing—that will result in what is called power. One inlet of power—the Holy Spirit in control."

~S.D. Gordon, 1904

INTRODUCTION

HIGHWAY OF HOLINESS

"A highway will be there, a roadway, and it will be called the Highway of Holiness."

-Isa. 35:8

The Spirit opened up a pathway for me to walk down in order to find my way back to the Lord. It was to lead me home both in the natural—to the house I grew up in where my parents still lived—and back into the church as well—the household of faith.

"For there is hope for a tree, when it is cut down, that it will sprout again, and its shoots will not fail. Though its roots grow old in the ground and its stump dies in the dry soil, at the scent of water it will flourish and put forth sprigs like a plant."

-Job 14:7-9

WELCOME HOME

Across the land, call it what you will
There's a river runnin', peaceful and still
And it flows on, makes its way down to the sea
It offers no resistance, it knows its [it's] gonna be

Welcome home, body and soul
Welcome home, we've all gotta go
Welcome home, father and son
Welcome home, you can hear the river run

Across the land, like a shadow on the hill
There's a storm a comin' up, that everyone will feel
And when it comes in, like a stranger in the night
It'll spoke the Spirit, till nothin' will set right

Welcome home, body and spirit
Welcome home, no you don't have to fear it
Welcome home, mother and daughter
Welcome home, we'll be safe on the water

Across the land, a multitude of dreams
Runnin' toward the river, like a million mountain streams
And they go on, with tomorrow on their side
Shinin' like the sun, on the sea at high tide

Welcome home, body and mind
Welcome home, I think we'll make it in time
Welcome home, future and past
Welcome home, home at last

(W. Berry / See & Say Songs, BMI)

Having come under the convicting work of the Spirit, I confessed my sin(s) and began the *process of repentance. In doing so, two key things sprang back to life in me. One was a reawakening of my prayer life. The other was a desire (hunger and thirst) for God's Word.

*Process of repentance: *"…repentance that leads to life."* (Acts 11:18)

"If we claim that we're free of sin, we're only fooling ourselves.

INTRODUCTION

A claim like that is errant nonsense. On the other hand, if we admit our sins—make a clean breast of them—he won't let us down; he'll be true to himself. He'll forgive our sins and purge us of all wrongdoing. If we claim that we've never sinned, we out-and-out contradict God—make a liar out of him. A claim like that only shows off our ignorance of God."
~1 Jn.1:9 - MSG

Repentance isn't just something we do after we've confessed our sin(s). The basic definition has to do with changing the way we think. In other words, it involves rethinking (or revising) how our thought processes work. To me, the application of pondering can be easily put into practice through the process of repentance.

Repentance is a way of life founded on our personal and/or corporate biblically-based understanding of Scripture and how we apply it to living as citizens of God's kingdom.

It is personal, but it can also be collective (i.e. corporate repentance). In other words, a person can repent, but so can a group, a congregation, or a nation. The principle and the practice are fundamental to a faith walk in Christ. Living in and for God's kingdom is impossible without such a purposed participation. At least I see it that way.

Regarding Corporate Repentance
(See 2 Chron. 7:14 / Neh. 9 / Dan. 9 / Acts 2)

A Disclaimer: I'm leaving out tons of details in this testimonial portion. For the most part, this section is intended to offer an overview of my sojourning in order to set the stage for my comments to follow in matters related to living life in the kingdom of God.

To continue...

Upon returning to, and being re-established in the church, I began to study the principles and precepts of Scripture with a desire to learn as much as I could about the ways of God, in order to grow in them, mature, and bear much fruit. As a result, I began to better understand and apply the principle of fruit-bearing in my service for the Lord.

"My Father is glorified by this, that you bear much fruit, and so prove to be My disciples."

-Jn. 15:8

I met, fell in love, and married Jean Marie—my wife of 39 years. Together, we were led to move to New York state where we enrolled in studies at Elim Bible Institute. The years we spent there were life-transforming to say the least. One thing in particular—one person in particular—deeply impacted my life during those training daze. I was able to take classes under the teaching leadership of Dr. Morris Smith. I credit him as being one of the first people to begin discipling me in matters related to kingdom living. His influence was a grace gift to me from the Father.

Dr. Smith had a unique anointing which helped him to take any topic he was addressing and transform it into a study of kingdom practices. I am still unpacking components of what he taught me almost 40 years ago. His impartations about kingdom matters introduced me to the topic I'll be addressing in the upcoming chapter. My deepest appreciation is extended to him for the service he showed me in his stewardship of what the Holy Ghost had given him to impart. I am eternally grateful for that. My quest for the kingdom began while I was at EBI.

INTRODUCTION

That quest is still an active part of my daily pursuits.

"You will seek Me and find Me when you search for Me with all your heart."
                                                                    -Jer. 29:13

Shortly after returning to Tennessee, and becoming an active member in a local church community, two books found their way into my life which changed things radically in regard to what later became known as the Praise and Worship Movement. They were, *The Hallelujah Factor* by Jack Taylor, and *Worship God: Exploring The Dynamics Of Psalmic Worship* by Ernest B. Gentile.

A great many books have impacted me over the years—a countless number really. However, those two became resources that shaped my personal theological understanding of praise and worship. In turn, those two inter-linked topics opened up a doorway that led me (and still leads me) further into matters dealing with the hows, and whys of living a biblically-based lifestyle which reflects God's kingdom here on earth, as it is in heaven.

Over the last four decades, I have transitioned from a student of the Word to a worship team member; worship team leader; and worship pastor. That process has brought me to now serve my Lord and His people as a teaching Levite. I am drafting this manuscript in that capacity, in order to continue fulfilling the charge on my life.

"He gave the priests detailed instructions and encouraged them in the work of leading worship in The Temple of God. He also told the Levites who were in charge of teaching and

> *guiding Israel in all matters of worship (they were especially consecrated for this), "Place the sacred Chest in The Temple that Solomon son of David, the king of Israel, built. You don't have to carry it around on your shoulders any longer! Serve God and God's people Israel. Organize yourselves by families for your respective responsibilities, following the instructions left by David king of Israel and Solomon his son."*
> ~2 Chron. 35:2-4 - MSG

This manuscript is a narrative endeavor directly linked with stewarding our citizenship in heaven, our ministry of reconciliation, our service as an ambassador of Christ, and our ability to become channels of God's very precious gift of grace.

Those responsibilities extend to *every* person we come into contact with, through either our personal relationships, or through the ordering of Divine circumstances, based on the sphere of influence that we've been given.

> *"But we will not boast beyond our measure, but within the measure of the sphere which God apportioned to us as a measure, to reach even as far as you.*
> *For we are not overextending ourselves, as if we did not reach to you, for we were the first to come even as far as you in the gospel of Christ; not boasting beyond our measure, that is, in other men's labors, but with the hope that as your faith grows, we will be, within our sphere, enlarged even more by you, so as to preach the gospel even to the regions beyond you, and not to boast in what has been accomplished in the sphere of another.*
> *But he who boasts is to boast in the Lord. For it is not he*

INTRODUCTION

who commends himself that is approved, but he whom the Lord commends."

~2 Cor. 10:13-18

I am not only a follower of Christ, I am also one of His disciples. As such, I am charged with helping to fulfill the so-called "Great Commission" given to disciples, in order to go and make more disciples.

"But Jesus came and spoke these words to *them, "All power in Heaven and on earth has been given to me. You, then, are to go and make disciples of all the nations and baptise them in the name of the Father and of the Son and of the Holy Spirit. Teach them to observe all that I have commanded you and, remember, I am with you always, even to the end of the world."

~Mat.28:18-20 - Phillips

*Them: Referring to 11 of His disciples (see verse 16)

From: The Unshakable Kingdom And The Unchanging Person

"In Matthew Jesus devoted a whole chapter to the kingdom of God, and in the midst of it he used a phrase, a disciple of the kingdom of God. This was illuminating and revealing. He had called them to be his disciples, but here he went further and called his disciples to be "disciples of the kingdom of God."

Here he put together these two things and made them one—to be his disciple was to be a disciple of the kingdom of God. To be his disciple was to be a disciple of his message, the Kingdom. He taught them many things, but he never asked his disciples to be disciples to anything except himself—nothing else, except the Kingdom. He identified himself and the Kingdom so completely that to be a disciple of one was to be a disciple of the other.

But here what God has joined together, man has put asunder. We have called men to be disciples of Jesus, but not disciples of the kingdom of God—to take the King but not his kingdom. This has weakened the impact of Jesus upon the world.

It is a personal relation of a person to a Person, but not a relationship with the order embodied in that Person. This was a vital loss, for the order was to be the life program of the disciple. Nothing can be compared with that loss, and nothing can be compared to the gain when we become disciples to the Kingdom."

~E. Stanley Jones, 1972

KINGDOM LIVING (Thoughts on Worship)

"Worship and obey the LORD your God with fear and trembling, and promise that you will be loyal to him."
~Deut.6:13 - CEV

JUST TO WORSHIP YOU

Far above the heavens, over all the earth
You O Lord, are worthy to be praised
Through the grace You've given
We come before Your throne
Seeking to behold Your face

INTRODUCTION

CHORUS:
Abiding in the shadow of Your Spirit
Hiding in the shelter of Your name
We have come by faith, Into this holy place
Just to worship You
Just to worship You
We are here just to worship You

Far above all rulers , authorities and powers
You O Lord, it's You alone who reigns
Through the grace You've given
We bow before Your throne
Honoring Your holy name

REPEAT CHORUS:

(W. Berry / See & Say Songs, BMI)

A life purposed and practiced in the kingdom cannot take place without a personal (and corporate) dynamic and redemptive component of worship being active in and among followers of Christ. I've addressed that subject in some detail in a chapter of my previous book. However, I think I need to make a few additional comments about it here as it inter-relates to the subject at hand—kingdom life.

Over the years, I've come across many definitions of worship. I've worked with and through several of my own as well. I have now (currently) condensed my thoughts down to this fundamental statement:

Worship is obedient service through self-sacrifice.

Here are two foundational expressions from Scripture which serve to support that definition:

In Gen. 22:5, we find the first usage of the word *worship*. In that context it means:

> To depress, i.e. prostrate (in homage to royalty or God); to bow (self) down, crouch, fall down (flat), humbly beseech, to reverence, make to stoop.
>
> (From *Strong's Concordance*)

There is a theological concept called the principle of first usage which applies here. Basically it states that how a word is used for the first time in Scripture is thereafter to be considered as the foundation on which any and all other usages of the same word (or its variations) are built upon.

The story in Gen. 22:1-5 gives us the first usage of the term (or concept) of worship. In that scene, Abraham tells his servants that he and his son Isaac *"will go over there; and we will worship and return to you."* (v.5).

The definition from *Strong's* presented above is how the word and its outworking should be understood in that context. The definition I used stating that worship is obedient service of self-sacrifice also grows out of what we're shown in the Gen. 22:1-5 text.

The New Testament expression of worship that Paul presents in Rom. 12:1, 2 is (from my perspective) directly linked to the same concept of obedient service through self-sacrifice. I'll include the rendering which Eugene Peterson provided us from the Message Bible here. It's the best word-picture I know of on the subject of worship under the New Covenant.

> *"So here's what I want you to do, God helping you: Take your everyday, ordinary life—your sleeping, eating, going-to-work,*

INTRODUCTION

and walking-around life—and place it before God as an offering. Embracing what God does for you is the best thing you can do for him. Don't become so well-adjusted to your culture that you fit into it without even thinking. Instead, fix your attention on God. You'll be changed from the inside out. Readily recognize what he wants from you, and quickly respond to it. Unlike the culture around you, always dragging you down to its level of immaturity, God brings the best out of you, develops well-formed maturity in you."

Peterson is saying we are to take every aspect of our life and *"place it before God as an offering."* The NASB says we are to, *"present our bodies as a living and holy sacrifice, acceptable to God, which is our spiritual service of worship."* The KJV says that doing so is our *"reasonable service."* The phrase *"reasonable service"* speaks from the original Greek as having to do with the very essence of worship.

Each rendering is saying that all of our life, the *"all that is in me"* (Ps. 35:10, Ps. 103:1-5, Ps. 150), is to be offered up daily to God as a living sacrifice of worship. I call that a "worship lifestyle." Personally, I can see no way of living in and living out the principles and precepts of kingdom life without a proactive approach to worship through reverence to the King of the kingdom—Christ Jesus.

Before I continue, I'll comment on what seems to be the contemporary understanding and practice of worship today. You may find it provocative. But, as I've already mentioned, provocation is part of what I do.

I must try and make this as clear as possible: My perspective regarding contemporary worship isn't based on contention or disagreement. Nor am I interested in taking sides in the so-called "worship wars." I'm not basing my position on style, taste, worship-team-presentations and the like. My intention here is to try and offer you a viewpoint based on how the kingdom of God is fashioned (designed), and grounded on how it is presented to us in Scripture. Said another way, I'm not looking for you to accept what I say as right and true. Rather, I'm attempting to share what the Holy Ghost has given me in regard to offering my life in obedient service as a sacrificial offering—which for me is worship.

> *"I ain't lookin' to compete with you, beat or cheat or mistreat you,*
> *simplify you, classify you, deny, defy or crucify you.*
> *All I really want to do*
> *is, baby, be friends with you."*
>
> ~B. Dylan

It seems to me that today's worshipping-church-at-large has moved a considerable distance away from the foundational definitions of worship found in the Bible (see Gen. 22:5 and Rom. 12:1, 2). Whereas the Old and New Testaments clearly state that worship can be seen as an event, the event is to be contained within a lifestyle of worship, not just in the event itself. In other words, the events are to be part of a worship lifestyle. They are to be encounters within the process of worship. A "worship experience" is not worship in total. Such "experiences" should be considered as components of worship. *There is a huge difference between attending a worship service and living life in the service of worship.*

Here's why. Basing worship on specific events can often lead directly to focusing on the "experience" of the event instead of the Person behind the events themselves. The very idea of evaluating a "worship service" as being a good one, or a bad one, has no basis at all in biblically-based theology.

Scripturally speaking, worship is to be grounded in self-sacrifice, not self-gratification! How one "feels" about worship isn't the point according to my understanding of the Word. The "why" of worship should be based on "Who" we worship. That is far more important than the "what" or "how" of it.

Our expressions of worship—in whatever form(s) they may manifest—should flow out of our relational willingness to offer it up from a place of yielded obedience as we live out *all* of our entire life as true (authentic) worshippers. That is lifestyle worship. That is kingdom life.

Please note that there is no mention of what we now commonly consider to be the components of worship in either the Gen. 22 passage, or the Rom. 12 passage. There is no singing of songs. There are no musicians, hymn books, or lyrics on projection screens. No dancing. No tongues. No clapping. No words of direction from the stage as to what the corporate body should be doing. Even though each one of those components has a role to play in corporate worship most certainly, they nonetheless are not mentioned in the two expressions I've shared from Scripture. Nope. The main thing we can draw from both those examples is that worship is heart and soul driven, birthed out of a willingness to be yielded through obedient service. And, to do so with *all* of one's life. That, dear cohorts, is worship as a lifestyle. And that sort of lifestyle is necessary (and reasonable) for those who are called to live as kingdom citizens.

{Selah...pause and ponder}

Watch how this works:

Virtually every aspect of one's life can be understood as being a particular component of worship when it's factored in as an act of self-sacrifice. Such self-sacrificing has to do with how one willingly yields over the aspects of life in regard to time, energy, thought (pondering, meditation), physical participation, and so on. When evaluated in those terms, anything and everything we do which contains a redemptive component can be expressions of worship. Prayer, fasting, time in the Word (for devotions, instruction, counsel, or teaching), sharing of one's personal energy, space, resources, etc., can be valued as obedient acts of service in and for God's kingdom. Related to in that way, all of life has the potential to be lived out as sacred.

Here are some verses for consideration and encouragement meant for worship pastors, worship leaders, worship team members, and worshippers "in the house" in general.

> *"That's when God set apart the tribe of Levi to carry God's Covenant Chest, to be on duty in the Presence of God, to serve him, and to bless in his name, as they continue to do today. And that's why Levites don't have a piece of inherited land as their kinsmen do. God is their inheritance, as God, your God, promised them."*
>
> ~Deut. 10:8 - MSG

> *"He gave the priests detailed instructions and encouraged them in the work of leading worship in The Temple of God. He also told the Levites who were in charge of teaching and guiding Israel in all matters of worship (they were especially consecrated for this), "Place the sacred Chest in The Temple that Solomon son of David, the king of Israel, built. You don't have to carry it around on your shoulders any longer! Serve*

INTRODUCTION

God and God's people Israel. Organize yourselves by families for your respective responsibilities, following the instructions left by David king of Israel and Solomon his son."
~2 Chron. 35:2-4 - MSG

"It's who you are and the way you live that count before God. Your worship must engage your spirit in the pursuit of truth. That's the kind of people the Father is out looking for: those who are simply and honestly themselves before him in their worship. God is sheer being itself—Spirit. Those who worship him must do it out of their very being, their spirits, their true selves, in adoration."
~Jn. 4:24 - MSG

In the KJV (*emphasis mine*), John 4:23 says:

"But the hour cometh, and now is, when the true worshippers *shall worship the Father in spirit and in truth..."*

If the text says there is such a thing as "true worshippers," and clearly it does say that, then it follows that there must also be a group of worshippers who are not "true" in regard to their approach, understanding, intent, or outworking of what they offer up. I read that passage like this: From among all the worshippers on earth, God is seeking for a specific kind—those who will worship Him *in spirit and in truth*. Let that soak in.

I WORSHIP ONLY YOU

CHORUS:
I worship only You, I worship only You

Worship is all we say and do
I worship only You

No, no, not money
No, no, not immorality
You're the true God only I worship only You

REPEAT CHORUS:

No, no, not power
No, no, not personality
You're the true God only
I worship only You

REPEAT CHORUS:
(Atlanta Metropolitan Cathedral - Composer Unknown)

An Axiom Cluster

A person who leads songs in church is a song leader.
A person who leads worship songs in church
is a leader of worship songs.
A person who leads worship songs in church
—having developed some personal understanding of
what worship is and how it is to be practiced—
is a worship theologian.
A person who carries worship in their head and heart
—with a desire to impart what they carry to both
individuals and congregations—
is a worship pastor.

PURPOSED PROSE

INTRODUCTION

"My heart bursts its banks, spilling beauty and goodness. I pour it out in a poem to the King, shaping the rivers into words."
~Ps. 45:1 - MSG

This is the second installment of my personal contemplations in matters related to life lived out within the kingdom of God. Pondering(s) #1 was published for two fundamental reasons:

1. To gather up data that I wanted to preserve for my family to have when I am no longer around.
2. To provide a resource for those who have requested that I gather up some of my teachings into a book which they could have as their own for study and teaching purposes.

The first installment was released in the U.S. in late '16. In March of '17, it was *launched in Johannesburg, and Durban in South Africa; also in Bulawayo, Zimbabwe. Where it's gone since then God only knows. So, I suppose that makes it an international publication, so to speak. (See 2 Cor.10:13-17)

On the African continent, newly-published books are acknowledged in a launching ceremony instead of being released.

This new edition contains additional data compiled from my personal theology. I am by no means a theologian by title or trade. However, I do have a set of core values that are built upon my understanding of God's Word, His ways, and His Divine will. How it all reads, and how readers relate to it remains to be seen. My responsibility is to try and present my observations as clearly and concisely as I can, in the hope that the seed I'm sowing will bear fruit in the lives of those who are pressing in and on up to Zion.

"And how blessed all those in whom you live, whose lives become roads you travel; They wind through lonesome valleys, come upon brooks, discover cool springs and pools brimming with rain! God-traveled, these roads curve up the mountain, and at the last turn—Zion! God in full view."

~Ps. 84:5-7 - MSG

DOING THE MATH (An Analogy)

"For He says, order on order, line on line, a little here, a little there. Indeed, He will speak to His people."

~Isa. 28:10

I'll mention a couple of things here regarding the biblically-based principle of seed sowing. The first is found in Psalm 126:5, 6. In that text, there are two specific things which characterize how seed sowing works.

"Those who sow in tears shall reap with joyful shouting. He who goes forth weeping, carrying his bag of seed, shall indeed come again with a shout of joy, bringing his sheaves with him."

~Ps. 126:5, 6

1. It impacts the sower by causing tears and weeping. In other words, it takes its toll emotionally on those who sow it.
2. There is a reward involved for the sower(s) based on the harvest which is to be reaped at the end of the process.

Note please that the joy is not in the sowing. That's where

INTRODUCTION

the tears and weeping take place. The joy comes at the harvest. Just to be clear here, that's not my interpretation of how the process works. That's clearly what the text says. Isn't it?

My second observation is based on the parable of the sower presented in Mat. 13:1-23. That passage has so much to consider contained in it. However, I only want to point out an aspect of it which relates directly to the process of seed sowing itself. I'll leave the other portions of the text for you to ponder on your own.

The text tells us there are four areas where seeds are sown and what the resulting yield is for each category.

Hard ground = No yield
Shallow ground = No yield
Weeded ground = Little yield
Good ground = Abundant yield

Now, suppose you were to divide all the seed into four equal parts and begin to scatter it all. Once that's done (mathematically speaking) there are now four ways for the seed to produce, or not produce as the case may be.

Based on the parable itself, it is likely that half the seeds won't produce any yield at all. Another ¼ may produce some small amount of yield—although that is certainly not a sure thing. However, the remaining ¼ will likely produce a substantial crop worth the effort to harvest.

That being the case (mathematically speaking) only ¼ of the seed sown may provide any reasonable return on the labor, tears, and weeping expended in order to later manifest as rejoicing when the harvest is gathered up (Ps. 126:6).

In light of that, there is a key lesson to be learned, and that is this: When we sow seed, we need to make sure we have lots of it to sow. Otherwise, our labors may turn out to be (more or less) in vain.

The narrative you're reading consists of seed. I am sowing it into whatever ground it may fall on. What happens with it thereafter is up to the one who receives it, and the Holy Ghost.

{Selah...pause and ponder}

"But you are the ones chosen by God, chosen for the high calling of priestly work, chosen to be a holy people, God's instruments to do his work and speak out for him, to tell others of the night-and-day difference he made for you—from nothing to something, from rejected to accepted."

~1 Peter 2:9, 10 - MSG

CHAPTER ONE
KINGDOM CITIZENSHIP

PROTOCOL AND PRACTICE

"Your testimonies are wonderful; therefore my soul observes them. The unfolding of Your words gives light; it gives understanding to the simple."

~Ps. 119: 129, 130

I've pondered long and hard about how to develop the theme of this chapter. I've come to the conclusion that the best course of action is to simply state (or restate) what my perspective is concerning God's kingdom. From there, I'll try to unpack how I arrived at such a position. So, here goes.

As I now see it, God's kingdom is *The Context* in which every single aspect of living as a follower of Christ is to be considered, contemplated, and carried out (Col. 3:17).

Without a context, things (aspects, components) can easily be considered as individual topics and not as pieces of a whole. Once that takes place, each separate part becomes a subject unto itself—random if you will. That doesn't necessarily diminish their value. Their importance can still be worthwhile in and of themselves. However, how each piece is related to the whole can then become overlooked, discarded, or lost altogether. Why? Because there is no context in place.

If something is to be considered in its proper (or fitting) context, several aspects need to be evaluated. Besides determining *what* something *is*, attention should also be given to the why, when, were, and how, along with the what. The specific thing itself may be the directed focus, but combining those other aspects will help to provide a proper context for it.

Such is the case when the kingdom of God is placed in its appropriate context. That context (as I now see it) is what holds [includes] all the other Biblical and Scriptural components of the Christian religion.

> **{Christian spirituality doesn't take place in a void, or a black hole. It is manifested throughout eternity in a never-ending universe of life and light.}**

Generally speaking, so many things which make up life itself would be more appropriately viewed and valued if context, where the foundational framework in which they are appraised, was applied.

This is how we fit into the context:

> *"For He rescued us from the domain of darkness and transferred us to the kingdom of His beloved Son, in whom we have redemption, the forgiveness of sins."*
> ~Col. 1:13, 14

That passage is addressed to those who have been reconciled to God, through their union with/in Christ Jesus, the Messiah,

Lord and Savior of all who have received Him as such—the *"first born among many brethren"* (Rom. 8:29c). Notice that the words *rescued* and *transferred* are both past tense—meaning that they have already transpired. A life that's been redeemed has already entered into the kingdom of God. However, there is a considerable difference between entering into it, and becoming acclimated into its full scope and scale.

Try looking at it this way: Let's supposed that the kingdom is a house, a very large one. We enter it through the doorway of Christ, *"the way, the truth, and the life"* (Jn. 14:6). Once inside, we find ourselves with two basis options as to what to do next. We can either position ourselves just inside the threshold of the doorway and live out our lives planted there until we die, and then enter heaven eternally.

Bear in mind that the only "experiences" we'll ever have camped out there will be limited to what our senses can perceive based on the atmosphere we find ourselves in within the environment surrounding us. Or, we can take the opportunity we've been graciously given to venture out into the rest of the rooms in the house, learning (experiencing) all we can regarding what and where we've entered. Such a grand adventure is exactly what we've been given as citizens of the kingdom of God's dear Son. (See again Col. 1:13, 14)

> *"In my Father's house are many rooms. If it were not so, would I have told you that I go to prepare a place for you?"*
> ~Jn. 14:2 - ESV

> *"They say in your father's house are many mansions.*
> *Each one has got a fire proof floor."*
> ~B. Dylan

Here are several quotes from Pastor Jack Taylor's book, *Cosmic Initiative*, which are important, insightful, and well worth inclusion here, regarding the subject at hand:

> "The Kingdom has come, the Kingdom is coming, and the Kingdom will come!"
>
> ~Taylor

> "The Kingdom is the whole into which everything else fits … it is relevant for the past, the present, and the future. It was the rule of God in the eternal past; it is the rule of God in the confusing present; and it will be the rule of God in the glorious future."
>
> ~Taylor

> *"…and He will reign forever and ever!"*
>
> ~Rev. 11:15

> "The Kingdom of God is not just one truth among many. It is *the* truth of truths—the truth that encompasses the collective body of truth. If it is anything, it is everything. If it matters at all, it is all that matters."
>
> ~Taylor

> "The Kingdom of God is the eternal rule of God over everything and everybody, everywhere, for all time and eternity. It is above time yet envelops time; it transcends time and endures time. It is the supreme reality—and the greatest theme in the universe.
>
> "Ultimate reality does not depend upon, and is not defined by visibility or tangibility but upon permanence.

In my view, the revelation of the Kingdom has almost completely disappeared from the eyes and ears of today's church."

~Taylor

"Developing a Kingdom mind-set begins with learning the nature of the Kingdom. A kingdom requires a sovereign ruler; those who are ruled; and rules."

~Taylor

"God is eternal, without beginning and without end; therefore His Kingdom is eternal."

~Taylor

"Human history's greatest truth, therefore, is the reality of the Kingdom of God on earth. We were designed by God, our Creator-King, to be children in His royal family, and to rule with Him in His Kingdom."

~Taylor

"What I'm trying to do here is to get you to relax, to not be so preoccupied with getting, so you can respond to Gods giving. People who don't know God and the way he works fuss over these things, but you know both God and how he works. Steep your life in God-reality, God-initiative, God-provisions. Don't worry about missing out. You'll find all your everyday human concerns will be met."

~Mat. 6:31-33 - MSG

"Jesus never declared, *Seek first...* about any pursuit or purpose except for the Kingdom of God. The Kingdom was the central message of His teaching and ministry on earth, and that of His disciples."

~Taylor

"Significantly, before Jesus returned to the Father in heaven, He spent forty days teaching His disciples about the Kingdom of God. (See Acts 1:3) The Kingdom continued to be His primary message, even after His resurrection."

~Taylor

Taylor sees the framework of the Kingdom of God as the central and significant context for God's eternal rule and its implications in every aspect of life on earth—and on into eternity. So do I. I agree with Taylor that a restored understanding of the Kingdom has implications for all arenas of life and will lead to these results and more:

- A renewed sense of purpose for individual believers
- A revitalized role for the church in the world
- The healing of society's ills
- The active proclamation of the gospel message with signs following
- A hopeful view of the future of humanity

A CONTEXTUALIZED APPLICATION

"The fundamental fact of existence is that this trust in God, this faith, is the firm foundation under everything that makes life worth living. It's our handle on what we can't see. The act of faith is what distinguished our ancestors, set them above

the crowd. By faith, we see the world called into existence by God's word, what we see created by what we don't see."
~Heb. 11:1-3 - MSG

As I've stated, God's kingdom is the context in which every single aspect of living as a follower of Christ is to be considered, contemplated, and carried out. Believing that to be the case, my comments (and supporting quotations) which follow hereafter in relationship to the Sermon on the Mount, the Beatitudes, the ministry of reconciliation, and ambassadorship for Christ, and living as channels of grace should all be appraised and applied within the context of the kingdom.

"Let every detail in your lives—words, actions, whatever—be done in the name of the Master, Jesus, thanking God the Father every step of the way."
~Col. 3:17 - MSG

The Sermon on the Mount provides the protocol for how the kingdom is to work (Mat. 5-7). The Beatitudes present the practical principles and precepts that we [as believers] are to live out of by faith (Mat. 5:1-12). From a broad-based viewpoint, we are to be extending the "ministry of reconciliation" [our job description] to *all* of humankind, serving as "ambassadors of Christ" (our job title). Doing so enables followers of Christ to live out their faith in the real world.

Drawing life from the capacity resident within our job description and our job title, we are empowered to advance God's kingdom here *"on earth as it is in heaven"* (See Mat. 6:10 and 2 Cor. 5:18-21). I'll address all this in more detail in the chapters that follow.

"The Sermon on the Mount has as its context the kingdom of God—it is an expounding of the laws, principles, and attitudes of the kingdom of God—it is vascular. *Cut it anywhere and it will bleed.* It is divine realism, a revelation of what God is, what the Kingdom is, as seen in Jesus, and what we can be like if we embody the Kingdom."

~E. Stanley Jones - Emphasis mine

"The most important thing Jesus said in the Sermon on the Mount was*: Seek first ye the kingdom of God…and all these things shall be added unto you* (Matt. 6:33). And the last thing he spoke to them was about the kingdom of God: *revealing himself to them for forty days, and discussing the affairs of God's Realm* (Acts 1:3 Moffatt). So first and last and between times the emphasis is upon the kingdom of God.

"And not a marginal emphasis, but the organizing emphasis upon which everything revolved and from which everything gets its meaning. Jesus preached the Kingdom as a mode of life now, a mode on which the total life, individual and the collective, is to organize, now."

~E. Stanley Jones

"The laws of the Kingdom of God are scattered throughout the New Testament. But there is one compendium of them so profound, comprehensive, explicit, imperial, that it may well be called, The Manifesto of the Kingdom. It is the so-called Sermon on the Mount."

The Kingdom: The Emerging Rule Of Christ Among Men
~George Dana Boardman

An Axiom
The New Testament is contained in the Old Testament.
The Old Testament is explained in the New Testament.

My comments here are not based on some new/profound revelation. Rather, after some 40+ years of praying, pondering, studying, processing and teaching kingdom concepts, the subject at hand is coming into focus for me with a clarity I've never experienced before. To a great extent, that is due to four books I've been working through over the last year or so. Those resources are:

Cosmic Initiative
by Jack Taylor
Whitaker House, 2017

The Unshakable Kingdom And The Unchanging Person
by E. Stanley Jones
Abigndon Press, 1972

The Kingdom
by George Boardman
Kessington Publishing, 2008 (originally published, 1899)

The Church
by George Boardman
Destiny Imaage, 2008 (originally published in 1901)

KINGDOM TRANSFORMATION

> "...we can be so sure that every detail in our lives of love for

God is worked into something good. God knew what he was doing from the very beginning. He decided from the outset to shape the lives of those who love him along the same lines as the life of his Son. The Son stands first in the line of humanity he restored. We see the original and intended shape of our lives there in him. After God made that decision of what his children should be like, he followed it up by calling people by name. After he called them by name, he set them on a solid basis with himself. And then, after getting them established, he stayed with them to the end, gloriously completing what he had begun."

~Rom. 8:28-30 - MSG

SET YOUR SIGHTS ABOVE
(Col. 3:1-3)

Set your affections on things above, and not on earthly things
For you have died and your life is hidden with Christ in God
So brothers be thankful, and let His word, dwell in your hearts with love
Share with each other, take care of each other
And set your sights above

If you are risen with Christ your Savior, then He is your all in all
And the peace of God, dwelling in your hearts
Is the peace to which you're called
So sisters be thankful, and let His word, dwell in your hearts with love
And whatever you do, let His Spirit show through
And set your sights above

Learn perfectness, through charity
Doing all in Jesus' name

Giving praise God, in thankfulness
Bringing honor to His name

Set your affections on things above, and not on earthly things
For you have died and your life is hidden with Christ in God
So brothers be thankful, and let His word, dwell in your hearts with love
Share with each other, take care of each other
And set your sights above
Share with each other, take care for each other
And set your sights above

(W. Berry / See & Say Songs, BMI)

"So [if] you're serious about living this new resurrection life with Christ act like it. Pursue the things over which Christ presides. Don't shuffle along, eyes to the ground, absorbed with the things right in front of you. Look up, and be alert to what is going on around Christ—that's where the action is. See things from his perspective."

~Col. 3:1-3 - MSG

"Set your [mind] on things above, not on the things that are on earth."

~Col. 3:2

There is a pre-condition placed on the verses above. That pre-condition is the word "if." That is to say, the charge in the text only applies to those who are *"hidden with Christ in God."* It has absolutely nothing to do with anyone who doesn't meet that pre-condition. It does not apply to unbelievers. Dear cohorts, think that through—it's an important concept to consider in terms of how we are to interact with those who are not of the faith. I'll unpack this in more detail in the next chapter on reconciliation.

To process and apply the directive to set our minds on things above is inter-related to how we put it into practice and what we expect from others in the process of doing so.

The word *mind* in the KJV means "affection." *Strong's* defines that word as follows: To exercise the mind. To be mentally disposed (in a certain direction). To interest oneself in (with concern to or obedience toward). *To think.* (emphasis mine)

The process of thinking is based more on education than it is on our intellect. It has more to do with what we learn, and less with increasing our I Q. The goal is (or should be) linked to developing knowledge, understanding, and wisdom in regard to living in God's kingdom. Merely filling up one's brain with data misses the point entirely.

> "…revelation is essential to the effectiveness of ultimate spiritual truth as far as its ability to change individuals and the surrounding culture. An intellectual grasp of biblical knowledge alone cannot enable us to participate with God to redeem lost humanity from the spiritual, social, and political devastation now being globally encountered. The church must rediscover the centrality of the Kingdom of God if it is to gain this needed revelation."
>
> ~Jack Taylor

An Axiom
Revelation to Transformation to Impartation

Revelation is first and foremost personal. One cannot impart their own personal revelation to anyone else. You can help provide an environment where revelation is possible to receive. However, you can't give yours away to others. They have to acquire their own.

Once a revelation is received, it has to take root and then bear fruit that manifests in the life of the recipient. In other words, it has to be owned by the person who received the seed. Thereafter, the revelation will (or should) continue to work transformation in the life of the person carrying it. The next phase in the process is that of releasing an impartation—a declaration if you will—in order for it to being part of a living testimony.

> "You have to say what you hear, so you can see what you say."
> ~Bishop Joseph Garlington

Revelation has to be internalized in order for it to effect change in the person who receives it (transformation). Thereafter it can serve as a catalyst for revelation in the lives of others (impartation).

Here's an example of how Scripture addresses such a process:

> "...*do not be conformed to this world, but be transformed by the* renewing *of your mind, so that you may prove what the will of God is, that which is good and acceptable and perfect."*
> ~Rom. 12:2 (Emphasis mine)

The word *renewing* in the Greek means *renovation*. From a word meaning *to renovate*. To renovate means to make new (with freshness). The transformation mentioned in that text has to do with learning or study, which in turn has to do with how we think about things of the kingdom—what those things are, and how to apply them to our daily lives.

Bear in mind that there are often (very often) Scriptural pre-conditions which apply to what we learn and how we put such learning into practice on a practical/experiential level.

> *"So Jesus was saying to those Jews who had believed Him, 'If you continue in My word, then you are truly disciples of Mine; and you will know the truth, and the truth will make you free.'"*
>
> ~Jn . 8:31, 32

I'll unpack those verses to show you what I mean:

The word *if* is conditional: *If* we continue in God's Word / The word *then* is conditional: we are truly disciples / Following that, the word *then* is implied again, coming after the word *and* / Thereafter, another conditional word *then* is implied once more following after the second use of the word *and*.

So, the text can be read like this:

If you continue in My word, *then* you are truly disciples of Mine; and *then* you will know the truth, and *then* the truth will make you free.

The entire sequence of events in that passage comes after the phrase, *"Jesus was saying to those Jews who had believed Him."* The word *believe* is the same word used in Jn. 3:16 along with many other places in Scripture.

What I've just shared about discipleship can be a subject of personal pondering for those of you who are prone in that direction. I go into more detail in my book, *Pondering(s)*, regarding the concept and dynamics of discipleship.

In the same way that salvation is a choice—based on so-called "free will"—so also is the choice to become a disciple. The choice to adhere to the teaching of Jesus as disciples is ours to make. However, the call to do so is conditional. Keep the *if* in mind. A resource for consideration about this is *The Great Omission* by Dallas Willard.

I'll just leave this here. Perhaps it'll *provoke* you to consider what you already know about the subject at hand—only now from an entirely different vantage point. How provocative is that?

STUDENTS OF THE WORD

"By Your words I can see where I'm going; they throw a beam of light on my dark path."
~Ps 119:105 - MSG

Recall please that we are to *"love the Lord with all our heart, soul, strength, and mind"* (Lu. 10:27). Therefore, the use of our minds in terms of loving the Lord is a biblically-based directive. The intent of that line of thought is not meant to be merely a mental exercise to improve our intellect. Rather the process of using one's intelligence is to be integrated into a full-orbed usage of who we are in Christ (heart/soul/mind/and strength). It is a *"with all that's in me"* concept. (Ps. 103:1)

2 Tim. 2:15 says,

"Be diligent to present yourself *approved to God as a workman who does not need to be ashamed, accurately handling the word of truth."

*The word *approved* in *Strong's* means *acceptable*. It comes from a word meaning "to be accounted as truthful in thinking or reputation."

Both Col. 3:1-3 and 2 Tim. 2:15 deal with the learning process (study). That means the charge of each text is that *all* believers are to become students of the Word. That being the case, then every believer should consider themselves students, which is what a *disciple is by definition. The call is there. So is the option.

*Disciple: A learner, pupil, student (*Strong's Concordance*)

The charge Paul places on those who are followers of Christ isn't intended for a select few as it is in the so-called "5 Fold Ministry" leadership giftings. In Eph. 4:11, we're told that those giftings were "given to some" for the "equipping of many" (NASB). Rather, the charge of being a workman who handles the word accurately is intended for any and all believers to put into practice. In other words, no Christian is exempt from finding ways to study to show themselves approved. At least not from a Biblical perspective. This is a stewardship issue—of our time and resources.

NOTE: When Paul speaks of *"rightly dividing the word"* (KJV) in 2 Tim. 2:15, he is referring to the Old Testament. Really? Why is that? Because the New Testament didn't exist when his letters were being written. Holy Scripture had not been canonized at that point in time. Therefore, his comments to those he was addressing—and to those who were to follow his teachings, like us—were to study the Old Testament. That right there will flat mess up a huge number of believers (including the leadership grouping in Eph. 4:11).

Any and all references in the New Testament that mention the use of scripture (i.e. the Word), are addressing the Old Testament (Torah). The New Testament didn't exist at the time the writings under the new covenant were being received and imparted.

Jesus' own words support the fact that the basis for the references regarding the use of the Word mentioned in the New Testament, are all addressing what's found in the Old Testament.

Christ said, *"...scripture cannot be broken..."* (Jn. 10:35b - KJV).

I'll repeat this axiom, because it applies here, and it's important to remember:

> The New Testament is contained in the Old.
> The Old Testament is explained in the New.

{Selah...pause and ponder}

Now, consider the term *due diligent* (what it means and how it works). The way we are to practice the concept of *"due diligence"* is the same way we are to *"study to show ourselves approved."* That in turn, links directly back to the Col. 3:1-3 passage in terms of where to focus our thinking and what to do with what we learn—being obedient by putting such knowledge into practice.

I'll just leave this here. Perhaps it'll *provoke* you to consider what you already know about the subject from an entirely different vantage point. How provocative is that?

WORDS ON THE WORD

"In the beginning was the Word, and the Word was with God, and the Word was God."

~Jn. 1:1

PONDERING(S) TOO

"Thy statutes are my songs in the house of my pilgrimage."
~Ps. 119:54

The contemporary church of the last 50 years or so has made the use of the word, *Word,* as a generic term for the Bible in a broad and generalized sense. What I mean is that we use the word, *Word,* to refer to pretty much any aspect of Scripture and leave it at that. Unless of course we are quoting a specific text or passage. When that's the case, we may provide a chapter and verse location. That is, if we happen to know it.

There is certainly nothing wrong with that practice such as it is. However, by doing so, I believe we tend to diminish the priority and power of The Book by speaking (and thinking) of it generically.

Our appreciation, reverence, and respect for the Bible may very well have been hollowed out (not hallowed out) by how we speak of it.

David, on the other hand, provides us with a personal testimony of how he revered the written word of God. His heart of love for it is presented in Ps. 119, which is a prayer of appreciation for what we today know to be the Old Testament. Here, I'll show you what I mean.

For the most part, every verse of David's testimonial in that lengthy Psalm uses a much deeper and wider vocabulary to express his heart-felt gratitude for holy rite. If you begin to unpack the language, you'll find that he uses eight different words for what we'd now simply refer to as God's Word. With each word David uses, he is identifying a particular aspect of the text and how he is impacted by it.

Consider the following words and their meanings:

Laws—A precept or statute; to point out (as if by aiming a finger)

Testimonies—To stand as a witness; to record; to duplicate or repeat

Commandments—o constitute; to set in order

Precepts—A mandate; to oversee or charge

Statues—A enactment (of labor or usage); to prescribe or decree

Judgments—A verdict; a sentence or formal decree; the exercise of justice

Word(s)—To speak, declare, decree; to talk or teach; to utter

Ordinances—A verdict; a formal decree; to measure or order into place

In Wayne-Speak, this is what I hear David saying regarding his love for, interest in, and adherence to the Word:

It stands as a witness, providing a model for us to learn from in order to repeat it through our own personal testimonies. It provides a set of constitutional directives to help us live orderly lives. It establishes precepts that are intended to have influence over our lives within a framework in which to abide. The practice of upholding judgment (of a Divine nature) is contained within what's stated. The very words it offers (its language and meaning) is intended to not only teach us how to live, but it also equips us to teach others based on how it is declared and decreed—which has at its root the practice of discipleship. It established a way to measure life lived out within a righteous and formal verdict, and thereby in the ordering of our conduct. Viewed that way, it is clear that we can/should be digging deeper into what Scripture has to say about conducting our lives from a biblically-based standpoint. Our kingdom citizenship is presented [in detail] throughout its pages.

All that links directly back into the subject of this chapter —kingdom citizenship. If our intention is to live in and out of God's kingdom, then we have to become knowledgeable of its constitution, its rules, its principles and precepts. The very protocol of how such a kingdom was designed to function requires us to pay attention to the handbook containing all the instruction needed to conduct ourselves as good citizens.

> *"By your words, I can see where I'm going; they throw a beam of light on my dark path."*
>
> ~Ps.119:105 - MSG

We are not required to memorize everything it says we are to do. However, we should adopt an understanding that sets it above a superficial acknowledgment of its so-called importance in our daily lives. In other words, the more importance we give the Word in terms of how we live, the better able we'll be in putting it into practice—living it out—as kingdom life.
"And the Word became flesh, and dwelt among us..."
~Jn. 1:14

Fleshing out the Word requires that we know it, and put it into practice.

NATIONALIZED CHRISTIANITY

> *"My kingdom is not of this world..."*
>
> ~Jn. 18:36a

Right here at the top of this sub-section, I want to make this as clear as possible—I am not addressing politics as such. My comments aren't intended to focus on right or left wingers, red or blue states, or the people who reside there. The only nation I'm considering is the one mentioned in 1 Peter 2:9 which states,

"But you are a chosen generation, a royal priesthood, a holy nation, *a people of God's own possession, so that you may proclaim the excellencies of Him who has called you out of darkness into His marvelous light."*

~Emphasis mine

I've chosen to deal with the nationalization of Christianity because I live in the USA, and most people who'll perhaps read my comments are Americans themselves. I could have used the title of nationalized religion as my heading. Really, any religion can in fact become nationalized if the concept from 1 Peter 2:9 is brought down to a temporal level by those who misunderstand, or misappropriate it, in order to fit it into a prioritized structure where the government they reside under here on earth becomes one that is placed over the *holy nation* that Scripture is referring to.

In a recent speech, French President Macron denounced nationalism as "a betrayal of patriotism," saying that "old demons are coming back to wreak chaos and death." He went on to state that people should "reject the selfishness of nations only looking after their own interest. Because patriotism is exactly the opposite of nationalism". As I've stated, I'm not addressing temporal governmental structures as such. I'm trying to focus you in on how the process of nationalism can impact anyone's religious beliefs and practices, in any nation, at any point in time.

Although Macron's comments were clearly intended to speak to the earth-bound dynamics within national governmental structures, that's not why I've included his remarks here. Note that although he was directing his words to governmental leaders and those they govern, he included a word which deals directly with the supernatural. The word is *demons*. In other words, he attributed what's taking place among the nations of the world directly to demonic activity. That's an astounding point for a national leader to put forth. By the choice of inserting that word, his proclamation moved from simply being a carnal observation to a spiritual concern. That's my point exactly.

When we choose (or allow) our earthly citizenship to override our eternal residency in God's kingdom, there is, as I see it, a huge spiritual deception at work. Are demons responsible for that? Perhaps so. At least it seems that the President of France is making a case for that possibility. I suppose you'll have to work all this out for yourself. I'll broaden what I'm saying out a little to help clarify my comments:

There are four basic components of life which are common to every person who has lived, is living now, or will live in the future that we have no control over, or say-so about. They are:

- When we were born
- Where we were born
- Who we were born to (or through)
- How we are physically formed

Those four aspects of our humanity should make it clear that nationalism as such cannot (or should not) be based on the mental, emotional, or cultural perspectives that we acquire as we move from birth to death. Here's why. Any national evaluations we hold to, based on the life span we have, are in and of themselves temporal—meaning they have an end. Whereas, the kingdom of God is eternal, having no beginning, middle, or ending. So, for those who consider themselves to be citizens of God's eternal kingdom (which is what the 1 Peter passage is speaking of), any aspect of one's national birthplace should be valued at some level underneath their heavenly and eternal homeland.

As Christians, we should hold to the viewpoint of being *"seated with God in the heavenlies."* (Eph. 2:4-7)

Not one of us has had any control or say-so in what nation we were born in, what era we were born into, along with its form of governmental structure. Nor have we been given any influence as to who our parents were, or how we were fashioned physically. Each of those components of life were of God's choosing. Therefore, our attachments in regard to each of them should be fundamentally based on how the Creator wants us to live our lives, in regard to His authority and Sovereignty.

> *"Oh yes, you shaped me first inside, then out; you formed me in my mother's womb. I thank you, High God—you're breathtaking! Body and soul, I am marvelously made! I worship in adoration—what a creation! You know me inside and out, you know every bone in my body; You know exactly how I was made, bit by bit, how I was sculpted from nothing into something. Like an open book, you watched me grow from conception to birth; all the stages of my life were spread out before you, The days of my life all prepared before I'd even lived one day."*
>
> ~Ps.139:14-16 - MSG

As I see it, there are two key portions of Scripture that should be viewed from their historical roots and then applied to our current age, in matters of how nations [and those living in them] are considered.

"I want you to get out there and walk—better yet, run!—on the road God called you to travel. I don't want any of you sitting around on your hands. I don't want anyone strolling off, down some path that goes nowhere. And mark that you do this with humility and discipline—not in fits and starts, but steadily, pouring yourselves out for each other in acts of love, alert at noticing differences and quick at mending fences. You were all called to travel on the same road and in the same direction, so stay together, both outwardly and inwardly. You have one Master, one faith, one baptism, one God and Father of all, who rules over all, works through all, and is present in all. Everything you are and think and do is permeated with Oneness."

~Eph. 4:2-5 - MSG

"In Christ's family there can be no division into Jew and non-Jew, slave and free, male and female. Among us you are all equal. That is, we are all in a common relationship with Jesus Christ. Also, since you are Christ's family, then you are Abraham's famous 'descendant,' heirs according to the covenant promises."

~Gal. 3:28, 29 - MSG

Both of those passages cut directly at the heart of nationalized religion. Why? Because they are addressing a *holy nation* from God's perspective, not ours. They both function outside of, above, and beyond earth-bound borders, racial discriminations, party lines, or homeland pride and/or prejudice. They deal with an eternal citizenship which transcends (or should transcend) our temporal loyalties and alliances.

Again I remind you that I'm not sharing my opinions, I'm

presenting my personal ponderings. My concern isn't that you agree or disagree with me. You have to make your own decisions in that regard. I'm only sowing some seeds. How (or if) they grow isn't up to me.

> *"It's not the one who plants or the one who waters who is at the center of this process but God, who makes things grow. Planting and watering are menial servant jobs at minimum wages. What makes them worth doing is the God we are serving. You happen to be God's field in which we are working."*
> ~1 Cor. 3:7-9 - MSG

Previously I shared some thoughts regarding the dynamics found in conditional "cause and effect" passages in the Bible. Such conditional aspects can be framed with either positive or negative effects.

By that I mean there can be a Scriptural statement that says if we do a certain something, then something good will follow. The other aspect is that if we don't do it—as directed by Scripture—something detrimental could happen to us. Here's one of my favorite verses which points that out:

> *"Therefore humble yourselves under the mighty hand of God, that He may exalt you at the proper time."*
> ~1 Peter 5:6

Our job is to humble ourselves. God's job (if/when He chooses to do so) is to exalt us. If we insist on doing His job, then He has no choice but to do ours.

So, we may find ourselves in negative circumstances where we begin to rebuke the devil out of the situation, thereafter only to find out that our rebukes aren't working. Perhaps we should first check ourselves to see how we are applying the dynamics of the cause-and-effect principle to the conditions we find ourselves in.

In the matter of nationalizing one's religion, consider how this oft-quoted passage can be misunderstood and misappropriated:

> *"[If] My people who are called by My name humble themselves and pray and seek My face and turn from their wicked ways, then I will hear from heaven, will forgive their sin and will heal their land."*
>
> ~2 Chron. 7:14

This is a cause-and-effect text which is clearly defined.

It opens with the conditional word, *If,* and continues to unfold from there. It states that there are three specific things to be done by those who consider themselves children of God, loyal subjects of His kingdom, His "chosen ones." (I Peter 2:9)

First, the text isn't addressing anyone who doesn't come under the covering of their Sovereign. Keep that in mind. Anyone and everyone who isn't part of that group of God-folk has no obligation to do what's being suggested. However, for those who are *called by His name*, it gives detailed steps to be taken in order to receive some specific things in return.

God's people are to:

1. Humble themselves
2. Pray
3. Seek His face
4. Turn from their wicked ways

If those things are done, then the second portion of the text becomes active. God will:

1. Hear from heaven
2. Forgive sin
3. Heal their land

Here again, the dynamic aspects of cause-and-effect have to be evaluated properly for the hoped-for results to come to pass.

Applying this text improperly is one way nationalism can begin to encroach upon and override the practice of living in and under a biblically-based government.

Note that the text doesn't prohibit God's folks doing any [other] specific things. So, to do them isn't a violation of Scripture as such. For example, a citizen of the U.S. could write letters, post up comments on line, get involved in street protests (or boycotts). Certainly voting would also be permissible in relationship to seeing our nation healed. However, though such things are not restricted, they are not what kingdom citizens are called to do biblically. Therefore, in order to hope to achieve the results presented in the text, the things to do are clearly stated. And, the downside is implied as well. In other words, regardless of whatever else we may attempt to do to see our land healed—a case can be made Scripturally that without doing the three key things the text tells God's people to do— He is not bound to do what the text says He will. Allowing a spirit of nationalism to become the priority that rises above kingdom protocol and procedure can result in the anticipated results never transpiring.

{Selah...pause and ponder}

WHO'S IN CHARGE HERE?

"For a child has been born—for us! The gift of a son—for us! He'll take over the running of the world. His names will be: Amazing Counselor, Strong God, Eternal Father, Prince of Wholeness. His ruling authority will grow, and there'll be no limits to the wholeness he brings. He'll rule from the historic David throne over that promised kingdom. He'll put that kingdom on a firm footing and keep it going with fair dealing and right living, beginning now and lasting always. The zeal of God-of-the-Angel-Armies will do all this."

~Isa. 9:6, 7 - MSG

Regardless of what your particular viewpoint is about the hows, whens, and whys of the kingdom of God, I think there is one fundamental question that should open such a discussion. It is this: In regard to God's kingdom, when does Sovereignty begin? Addressing that question on the front end could certainly help to provide a perspective from which to try and develop one's theology related to kingdom matters.

Sovereignty: 1. Supreme excellence, or an example of it, 2.a. Supreme power over a body politic, b. freedom from external control, c. a controlling influence.

~Webster's Dictionary

For me the subject of sovereignty in kingdom matters is easily settled. Since the kingdom of God is eternal (without beginning, middle, or end), then the sovereign reign of whomever is in charge isn't in and of itself an issue of time.

Therefore, the Isa. 9 passage is an eternal statement that is working itself out on earth according to earth time. In other words, the Sovereign position is already in place (since before time began). It's just not manifesting in all its fulness yet.

That being the case, from a governmental perspective, who is in charge of the governmental system that Christians are subjects of depends on what kingdom they identify with as their top priority. Who do they co-operate with, and serve? (See Deut. 5:7).

If a follower of Christ is also to be an ambassador for Christ, then how our government functions should be determined by our Sovereign allegiance. Since our Sovereign is—Sovereign— He makes the rules and establishes the protocol to follow as He determines. It is up to those under His rulership to submit to and live within such a framework.

> "Although we were designed and commanded to reign over God's entire creation, it must be understood that this reign has always been predicated on His reign over us. His sovereignty in our lives is what gives us reigning privileges and responsibilities."
>
> ~Taylor

There is a wonderful resource which deals with that subject in a very insightful and creative way. It's titled, *The Most Important Person On Earth*, written by Dr. Myles Munroe. If you're finding this topic regarding governmental structure of interest, I highly recommend that you purchase it and work through it for yourself.

Here is an excerpt from the introduction, titled "Kingdom Government."

"The original blueprint of the Creator was for a kingdom government on earth as an extension and reflection of his own greater, spiritual kingdom. This earthly government was to be a thriving colony with humanity as (1) its citizens, and (2) its local vice *governors representing the home kingdom. Our mandate was to transform the colony into the nature of the kingdom."

*For the purposes of this manuscript, I'd substitute the term *ambassadors* for *governors*. I'll address that in Chapter 3.

Dr. Munroe's book uses the role of the Holy Spirit as an example to show how governorship is fashioned to work in terms of overseeing a state, region, or nation. Although a governor and an ambassador are not exactly the same in terms of their respective roles, they are nonetheless similar. They are both charged with establishing and manifesting a model of representation for people groups to yield to and function under.

Such a modeled role for the Holy Spirit was stated by Jesus when he told his disciples;

"But the Helper, the Holy Spirit, whom the Father will send in My name, He will teach you all things, and bring to your remembrance all that I said to you."

~Jn. 14:26

"...I tell you the truth, it is to your advantage that I go away; for if I do not go away, the Helper will not come to you; but if I go, I will send Him to you."

~Jn. 16:7

According to Scripture(s), the Holy Spirit is therefore our

governing agent (our kingdom representative) for conducting life here on earth, as it is in heaven.

The same power that is resident and available in the Holy Spirit, is in fact the very same power which is accessible and applicable for those who are in Christ. Indwelled and empowered in such a way, the ability to both be a witness and declare testimony mentioned in Acts 1:8 is a task which can be accomplished in service of God's kingdom. Our job assignment is achievable when the manifested and empowering presence of the Lord is abiding in us, and working through us.

Presence + Power = Witness and Testimony

I see yet another example of inter-linkage between what the Father gave to the Son, and then by extension, is given to those who are joined with Him.

Consider this:

"Ask of Me, and I will surely give the nations as Your inheritance, and the very ends of the earth as Your possession."
~Ps. 2:8

The seeds of the plan for the ministry of reconciliation are contained in that passage. Christ Jesus nurtured them in the so-called *Great Commission* given to His disciples:

"And Jesus came up and spoke to them [disciples], *saying, 'All authority has been given to Me in heaven and on earth. Go therefore and make disciples of all the nations, baptizing them in the name of the Father, and the Son and the Holy Spirit, teaching them to observe all that I commanded you,*

and lo, I am with you always, even to the end of the age.'"
~Mat.28:18-20 (Addition mine*)*

At least I see them there. Notice that the gift of the nations isn't imparted from the Father to the Son in order to nationalize them all under Christ heavy-handed-dictatorial-authority. Most certainly not. That's not the case at all. Rather, the nations are reconciled to Jesus through the act itself, as the text below states:

"Now all these things are from God, who reconciled us to Himself through Christ and gave us the ministry of reconciliation, namely that God was in Christ reconciling the world to Himself, not counting their trespasses against them…"
~2 Cor.5:18, 19a

The inheritance Abba Father gave His Son, Christ Jesus, is ours to share as well. For, in Christ, we are:

"…heirs also, heirs of God and fellow heirs with Christ…"
~Rom.8:17

PLEASANT PLACES
(Ps. 16:3, 4)

CHORUS:

Pleasant places, pleasant places
The boundaries of my life, have fallen in pleasant places
Pleasant places, pleasant places
Provision from God's hand, enables me to stand
In these pleasant places

Holy expectations, Divine anticipation
A kingdom revelation of what waits up ahead
The glory and the splendor, in the Presence of my Savior
Reminds me of the words the Psalmist said (He said)

REPEAT CHORUS:

My inheritance is beautiful to me
Oh my Lord, I have no good but Thee
And my inheritance is beautiful to me

                                    (W. Berry / See & Say Songs, BMI)

Dr. Munroe continues:

> "To fully appreciate the invisible kingdom government, we must realize that the idea of 'kingdom' didn't originate on earth with the ancient civilizations of Babylon and Egypt. It didn't come from earth at all. The concept of kingdom is rooted in the desire of The Creator to design and sustain both the unseen and seen reals in order to express, represent, and manifest his nature."

That too speaks of the charge I've already mentioned regarding the 2 Cor.5:18-21 charge on the lives of *every* believer.

Then, from the section titled, "The Concept Of The Kingdom" he says this:

> "The word *king* refers to the person or personality who influences and oversees the productive development and profitable service of everything under his care, for the fulfillment of his noble desires and the benefit of

all those living in his realm. The environment, territory, and authority over which he presides are his 'domains' or 'realms.' A king effectually relating it his domains is the essence of the concept of kingdom.

Kingdom is thus the perfect example of the divine, creative act of the Creator. The first realm of his dominion is described as heaven. Heaven is the original kingdom; it was the origin of kingdoms. No kingdom existed before it, and nothing natural can be adequately compared to it. It is the first real kingdom because the first King created it. The kingdom of heaven is the only perfect prototype of kingdoms in existence.

When our Creator-King desired to extend his perfect kingdom from the invisible realm to the visible realm, the result was the creation of the physical universe and the appointment of planet earth as the destination for a unique extension of his divine being. Paul of Tarsus attempted to communicate this divine process of creation and extension when writing to people in the city of Colossae: *By him all things were created: things in heaven and on earth. Visible and invisible, whether thrones or powers or rulers or authorities; all things were created by him and for him.*

The kingdom of heaven and its colony of earth exist through the will of our Creator-King. It is therefore impossible to comprehend humanity's purpose without understanding the kingdom concept and how we are meant to live it out on earth. An inter-realm connection through the Holy Spirit is what enables us to fulfill our very purpose as human beings. The kingdom government is the ultimate answer to our search for personal significance and the meaning of the world around us."

Now those are some provocative insights right there!

"There are no nations in Jesus Christ's outlook, but the world."
~O. Chambers

Nationalism and patriotism are not the same thing. Defined in *Webster's* they are as follows:

Patriotism is loyalty or devotion to a nation.

Nationalism is a sense of national consciousness exalting one nation above all others and placing primary emphasis on promotion of its culture and interests as opposed to, or at the expense or exclusion of, other nations or supranational groups.

For Christians, it is my personal belief that patriotism is appropriate when held under (or in submission to) the kingdom of God. Nationalism, on the other hand, has no place in matters related to the life and lifestyle of those who are stationed here to represent God's kingdom *"on earth as it is in heaven."*

Believers all over the earth use the Biblical language and titling of "King of kings, and Lord of lords" over and over and over. Those titles are outworkings of the Deut. 5:7 directive that kingdom citizens are to have *"no other gods before Me."* The exaltation of and yielding to such titles can only be authentically lived out in the lives of Christians when priorities are clearly defined in terms of whose headship has our allegiance and our loyalty.

The issue of how our kingdom citizenship gets sorted out here on earth isn't anything new. It's not a contemporary quandary that has arisen in the last generation or two. Followers of Christ were confronted by the same situation when He was living among them. His disciples had this to say:

> *"So when they had come together, they were asking Him, saying, "Lord, is it at this time You are restoring the kingdom to Israel?"*
> ~Acts 1:6

The kingdom of God is here now. It's among (or available to) everyone on the planet (See 2 Cor.5:19). It's resident inside of those who believe. It's ever advancing, and therefore it's every manifesting. But, at this moment in earth-time, it is not visibly evident for all humanity to see. It was not, is not, and will never be restricted by the temporal concept or formation of any national government. The Christian faith is (or should be) lived out eternally, within the context of a life lived in and for the kingdom of God. Kingdom life *por vida*!

When we attempt to make the eternal temporal, we diminish the supernatural. Once that happens, the dynamic attributes of God's manifest presence and power are lacking within as well as outside of the church-at-large.

THE DOWNSIDE OF DOUBLE-MINDEDNESS

> *"Study to show yourself approved to God…"*
> ~2 Tim.2:15

The power manifestation of Acts 1:8 was fashioned in such a way as to energize witnesses to carry "the gospel of the kingdom" (Mat.24:14) throughout the earth. That power is an extension of God's Sovereign presence embodied in and through the Holy Ghost.

> *"But the Holy Spirit will come upon you and give you power. Then you will tell everyone about me in Jerusalem, in all*

Judea, in Samaria, and everywhere in the world."
~Acts 1:8 - CEV

Presence proceeds power. Power produces witness. Witness proclaims testimony. Testimony provides kingdom expansion.

When we allow any of the temporal government(s) on earth to supplant or override the eternal truth(s) of God's headship, we are nationalizing religion. It follows thereafter that such nationalization (dare I say it, Americanization) then becomes a major distraction in regard to where our loyalties are to be placed as citizens of heaven. Potentially, we can then end up with a divided heart. Or, if you will, we can become "double-minded," or of a split-spirit.

"A double-minded man is unstable in all *his way."*
~Ja. 1:8 (Emphasis mine)

From *Strong's Concordance*, *double-minded* means two-spirited, i.e. vacillating (in opinion or purpose).

In Wayne-Speak, that verse says that *all* people who are double-minded are "two-spirited," vacillating back and forth in *all their ways*.

Now, just ponder that concept for a moment as you survey the world around you. That's how millions of people function on a daily basis all over the planet. You may be one of them.

In a very real sense, the unstable state of things among humanity has its root-base in being double-minded in terms of who's in charge, and what our responsibility is to Who that is.

"Thou shalt have no other gods before me."
~Deut. 5:7 (Emphasis mine.)

The NASB offers an alternative rendering of the verse in its notes.

"You shall have no other gods beside *Me."*
~Deut. 5:7 (Emphasis mine.)

I much prefer that interpretation of that text. Here's why:

To me, it more clearly states the intent of the content. It excludes any and all other little gods, leaving those who follow Christ with the biblically-based charge to make sure Who we are serving on a singular basis.

The verse states that there are [in fact] other gods which can draw us away from where our kingdom alliances are to be held securely. However, the gods mentioned are presented with a lower-case *g* as well as a plural *s*, i.e. gods. Meaning there are more than one, but none of them are Sovereign.

The text is acknowledging that other gods do exist (small *g* and plural). But, it tells us that they are not to have a place in our lives which undermines our relationship of yielded and obedient submission to the "One True God." (Ps. 115)

Dear cohorts, that's exactly what takes place when we allow nationalization of our religion to take hold in our hearts and minds. Doing so can also lead to our souls being taken captive and held hostage as well.

OH GOD (YOU ARE MY GOD)

(Ps. 63)

On God, You are my God, and I will forever praise You
Oh God, You are my God, I will place no other God above You
In a dry and weary land where there's no water

I will build myself a stronghold out of praise
I will lift up holy hands before You, Father
And I will worship You for all Your awesome ways

Underneath the shadow, underneath the shadow of Your wings
(I will hide myself)
Underneath the shadow, underneath the shadow of Your wings
(I will sing for joy)
Underneath the shadow of Your wings

(W. Berry / See & Say Songs, BMI)

As I've stated, this is not a new issue. Not at all.

A PROFOUNDLY PROPHETIC PRONOUNCEMENT:

In 1899, George Boardman published a work that is now considered a classic in Christian literature titled *The Kingdom: The Emerging Rule Of Christ Among Men*. For historical context, that was 120 years ago, 35 years after the Civil War. Reading it is overwhelming—it is undoing me. What follows is his commentary on an aspect of living the Christian life, having to do with hiddenness (see Phil. 2:5-8 - MSG). Although some of the language presents words we rarely (if ever) use anymore, I'm quoting it just as it was written—because it is so beautiful in its narrative:

> "The Christian life is a secluded life, not in the monastic sense of bodily isolation (for what is monasticism but a life intensely ostentatious and scenic?), but in the sense of modest reserve or spirit bashfulness. To take, then, this hidden life from out of the sequestered bowers, recesses, and Shrines which are its native home, and bring it out

into the garish day, and put it through a parade drill, is to expose it to all manner of peril, either vaporizing in into unconscious self-deceit, or freezing it into conscious hypocrisy. No; the life in Christ, like Christ himself, neither strives nor shouts, nor does anyone hear its voice in the streets. It shrinks from all displays, whether ostentatious alms giving, or conspicuous devotions, or ceremonious fasting, or broadened phylacteries, or processional parades, or advertisements of baptisms, or clerical costume and badges and titles, or ostentatious kneelings, or protruded orthodoxy of creed, or holy tongues, or cants of evangelic brogue. Like planet around sun, it rolls in its orbit of obedience without parade; like the sun itself, it shines without noise."

Remember that this quoted section was written 120 years ago.

"This mandate of unostentation is in a special degree suited to us Americans. Publicity is to a painful degree the bane of American piety. It is a day of nervous running to and fro, and Martha-like distraction about much serving; a day of organizations, conventions, anniversaries, public meetings of all sorts. It has almost come to be understood that we can do nothing for God and His kingdom unless we organize and hold a public meeting. Private worship has thus largely given way to public: the closet to the synagogue. Let us take care lest this demonstrative piety of ours lead into Pharisaic ostentation and issue in Pharisaic hypocrisy.

Let us beware of this promiscuous, outdoor, garish life, where the café supplants the closet. Let the modesty of Nature be to us a parable. Her reservoirs are subterranean."

Commenting on the beatitude which says, *"Blessed are the meek for they shall inherit the earth"* (Mat. 5:5), George Boardman had this to say in 1899:

> "Beware, my countrymen, how you allow yourselves to be beguiled into territorial expansion by the blustering talk about the certainty of American domination or 'manifest destiny.' Earth's majesties are no match for the King's meek ones."

Boardman continues stating;

> "'Blessed are those who hunger and thirst after righteousness' (Mat. 5:6). All souls are made to crave. We crave for husks as well as for manna. Righteousness is the only food that can meet this craving—the righteousness of actual character, the righteousness of doing the King's will personally, consciously, joyously; the righteousness of personal perfectness, even as our heavenly Father is perfect: this is the righteousness, and this only, which can satisfy the soul's true hunger."

Then he adds;

> "'...for they shall be filled.' The righteous soul's growing volume ever demands a growing volume of food; and the hunger for any given stage will be duly met at that stage. Demand and supply, so disproportioned in this world's economics, are correlatives in the Kingdom of God."

Stunning (and timely) insights!

CHAPTER TWO
MINISTERS OF RECONCILIATION

"He has committed to us the word of reconciliation."
~2 Cor. 5:19c

From *Strong's Concordance*: *Reconciliation* is defined as an exchange (adjustment); restoration to (the divine) favor. From a word meaning to change mutually; to compound a difference.

TIME MANAGEMENT

"Teach us to number our days, that we may present to You a heart of wisdom."
~Ps. 90:12

Time is a construct, created by God to frame (contain) human history, along with everything else that takes place on the earth. Since eternity is not bound by earth-time as such, having no beginning or ending, time's earthly framework has no direct bearing on what takes place in eternity. Eternity was, is, and will be. Earth-time only exists to provide a container for events which have happened, are happening, and will happen on this planet in the future. Eternity does not respond to earth-time as such, since it takes place outside of it.

PROVOCATION IN ACTION

"In the beginning..."

~Gen. 1:1

In the matter of time, the most important word in that phrase from Gen. 1:1 is *beginning*. Here's why. God was moving from within eternity, which has no beginning, to establish the very existence of time itself. He created it to provide a context for what He intended to do on the earth. During the act(s) of creation, He set in place a framework from which time could unfold.

Day #1 and following presents us with a defined measurement. Regardless of what your personal perspective is concerning creation theology, it is clear from Scripture that each day was measured by a specific construct of time—having both a beginning as well as an ending.

"From the rising of the sun, till its going down..."

~Ps. 113:3

Here are two Biblical statements that reflect the biblical history of how people have understood life in terms of time since it began: *"My times are in Your hand..."* (Ps. 31:15) and *"Teach us to number our days..."* (Ps. 90:12). Those are both Old Testament perspectives. The New Testament shares a similar

POV when it says, *"while it is still called today..."* (Heb. 3:12-15 - MSG). Here's another;

> *"But when the fulness of time had come, God sent forth His Son, born of a woman, born under the Law, so that He might redeem those who were under the Law, that we might receive the adoption as sons."*
>
> ~Gal. 4:4

There are so many Scriptures which address the subject of time. But, for now, those four give us a foundation upon which to build our own theology regarding the subject of time—where it came from, why it was fashioned, and what to do with/about it until it ends. I'll come back to the Gal. 4:4 text again later to consider it in more depth.

To recap—regarding time and history—stated simply: God created time to provide a context for what He intended to do on the earth. At least that's how I currently understand the subject being addressed.

Having said all that, a question arises that needs consideration. After God created time, what did He then intend to do? Scripture tells us:

> *"Let us make man in our image..."*
>
> ~Gen. 1:26

RELATIONAL UNITY

> *"I don't want any of you sitting around on your hands. I don't want anyone strolling off, down some path that goes nowhere. And mark that you do this with humility and discipline—not*

in fits and starts, but steadily, pouring yourselves out for each other in acts of love, alert at noticing differences and quick at mending fences. You were all called to travel on the same road and in the same direction, so stay together, both outwardly and inwardly. You have one Master, one faith, one baptism, one God and Father of all, who rules over all, works through all, and is present in all. Everything you are and think and do is permeated with Oneness."

~Eph. 4:3-6 - MSG

UNITY

(Ps. 133)

Behold how good and pleasant it is
When believers are dwelling in unity
It's like the dew of Hermon, coming down on Mt. Zion
When the people of God see their destiny

BRIDGE:
There the Lord commands a blessing
When He hears us all rejoicing
In the bond that's been created
Through the blood of our Redeemer

CHORUS:
(He gives us) life forevermore
Life forevermore, life forevermore
When we are united in Him

Behold how good and pleasant it is
To be seated with God in the heavenlies

*It's like the dew of Hermon, coming down on Mt. Zion
And washing away our iniquity*

REPEAT BRIDGE and CHORUS:
                                        (W. Berry / See & Say Songs, BMI)

The Trinity is relational—The Father, Son, and Holy Ghost—Three in One. The interaction between those three Persons is total, complete, and inter-connected eternally. A case can therefore be made stating that relationships are a fundamental aspect of eternal life. Relationship(s) are not only inspired and modeled by the Trinity, they are also [perhaps] the fundamental reason that humankind came into being in the first place.

Consider Ps. 133 as it relates to the subject of unity:

"Behold how good and how pleasant it is for brothers to dwell together in unity! It is like the precious oil upon the head, coming down upon the beard, even Aaron's beard. It is like the dew of Hermon coming down upon the mountains of Zion; for there the Lord commanded the blessing—life forever."
                                                              ~Ps. 133:1-3

If the Trinity said, *"Let us make man in our image,"* then it must (at its foundational base) be intended to establish interaction between humankind and the Trinity. The establishment and unfolding of the very first relationship(s) between man (Adam and Eve) and the Creator is presented to us in Scripture beginning at the creation of man and continuing up until The Fall.

When sin entered the world, the plan for re-establishing a relationship between God and man was introduced (Rom.

5:12-21). That plan was reconciliation (2 Cor. 5:18-21), or, if you prefer, the Gospel, the Good News. That plan was already in place in the mind of God before it was ever introduced on earth. It was formulated in the mind of God in eternity, outside of earth-time. Therefore, it is an eternal plan.

That concept is filled with mystery. Since God is Omniscient—having infinite awareness, understanding, and insight—He knew what was going to take place regarding The Fall prior to it happening. It did not alter His plan. Rather, it set it into motion within the context of time.

{Selah...pause and ponder}

"But when the fullness of the time came, God sent forth His Son, born of a woman, born under the Law, so that He might redeem those who were under the Law, that we might receive the adoption as sons. Because you are sons, God has sent forth the Spirit of His Son into our hearts, crying, 'Abba! Father!' Therefore you are no longer a slave, but a son; and if a son, then an heir through God."

~Gal. 4:4-7

"Paul urged us to be 'eager to maintain the unity of the Spirit...until we all attain to the unity of the faith and the knowledge of the Son of God...' (Eph. 4:3, 13). Christian unity is not unity in what we believe or what we know about Jesus. It is unity of the Spirit. I have close friends who are committed to doctrines I cannot agree with, but we experience unity in the Spirit. We have different ideas about how to 'do church,' but we worship Jesus Christ, the Son of God. Unity of the faith and 'mature manhood' (Eph. 4:13) are yet to come. Strive to maintain unity."

~Fount Shults

"Whatever you may believe about the Genesis account of creation the emphatic portion is that God and man have a kinship—they are not alien, they are affinities; the same laws of character are in God and man; the kingdom of God is man's native land; man is built to obey and enjoy that kinship; it is man's native land; it is man's natural way to live. Human nature itself is fulfilled when it obeys the laws of the kingdom of God. When we obey the laws of the kingdom of God we are obeying the laws of our own being. It is the natural way to live."

~E. Stanley Jones

Here's a quote expressing how reconciliation is outworked:

"When that kind of love is working, then it includes people of every kind, and you have a growing assembly of people who are included in delighting in Jesus…

When you fall out of love with selfishness, out of love with pride, out of love with self-pity, out of love with anger, out of love with self-exaltation, needing to have your own way all the time—when you're falling out of love with that and falling into love with Jesus, who laid down his life for others, your whole life takes on an expansive quality.

It starts to have an impulse of: 'I want you in. I want you in here. Come on in. This is the greatest thing in the world. I want as many people in as possible … the more diverse, the more radiance shines from the diamond they're all admiring.' And so you're not hindered by ethnicity or class or gender or whatever. You want everybody you know—every human being included … your heart has been so altered by being satisfied with the way Jesus is that you want others in."

~John Piper

RELATIONAL DISCONNECT (The effects of The Fall)

"You know the story of how Adam landed us in the dilemma we're in—first sin, then death, and no one exempt from either sin or death. That sin disturbed relations with God in everything and everyone, but the extent of the disturbance was not clear until God spelled it out in detail to Moses. So death, this huge abyss separating us from God, dominated the landscape from Adam to Moses. Even those who didn't sin precisely as Adam did by disobeying a specific command of God still had to experience this termination of life, this separation from God. But Adam, who got us into this, also points ahead to the One who will get us out of it."

~Rom.5:12-14 - MSG

"When man fell—he sinned against the kingdom of God and sinned against the laws of his own being. We call that the Fall. But the Fall does not mean the obliteration of the image of God.

The laws of the kingdom of God are still the laws of the being on fallen man … evil is living against the laws of God written in his own being, and he is still made by God and for God and hence he feels divided, at war with himself, when he is living a life of sin ... as we unfold the laws, principles, and attitudes of the kingdom of God as seen in the Sermon on the Mount, I believe we will be astonished at the sheer sanity of the kingdom of God ... the only thing that holds this civilization together is the leaven of people who, within the Church and outside the Church, are living in kingdom ways...the rest pull it apart by their un-kingdom ways ... is this the partisan view of a partisan?

Well, I am a partisan, a convinced partisan, driven to this partisanship by observing how life is lived in East and West, North and South, for over half a century—lived in un-kingdom ways and in kingdom ways. The difference is a difference between darkness and light, between insanity and sanity."

~E. Stanley Jones

Before I address the subject of reconciliation, I need to say something else about the kingdom of God. To do so, I'll focus on two concepts:

- Principle: A goal to achieve (as in trying to reach the top of a mountain)
- Precepts: The pathway(s) that can be taken to help reach an intended goal

Any given principle intended to be reached can have more than one pathway toward accomplishment. But, each pathway must keep the specific goal in sight. (See Ps. 84:5 and note that the word *highways* is plural. Also see Isa. 12:3 and note that the words *wells* or *springs* are also plural.)

Stated simply, we can reach our goal (principle) by following the pathways/streams (precepts) that will lead us there.

Now, stay with me here, this slope gets a little slippery: If the goal (principle) we're trying to reach is to live in and help establish/expand God's kingdom, *"on earth as it is in heaven"* (Mat. 6:10), then each and every pathway (precept) presented to us in Scripture is there to lead us directly to our goal. The catch is that we must do two key things to reach our goal.

- Learn what the precepts are
- Learn to follow the pathway(s) in obedience to the desired destination (principle)

If we choose to take other paths which lead us away from those presented in Scripture, we will end up off course, missing our intended goal. That's exactly why conviction, confessing, repentance, restoration, renewal, and (wait for it) reconciliation are all made available to us as followers of Christ. They provide co-ordinates for our GPS (Gospel Positioning System). Precepts of conviction, confession, repentance, restoration, renewal and reconciliation are all given to us to help us reach our goal—life lived in and of the Kingdom. I hope I didn't lose you somewhere along this trail.

> *"And how blessed all those in whom you live, whose lives become roads you travel; they wind through lonesome valleys, come upon brooks, discover cool springs and pools brimming with rain! God-traveled, these roads curve up the mountain, and at the last turn—Zion! God in full view!"*
>
> ~Ps .84:5-7 - MSG

It's a "long obedience in the same direction."
~Eugene Peterson quoting Friedrich Nietzsche

An Axiom
Vision—Where we're going
Mission—How we intend to get there
Goals—Markers along the way which help determine progress (or lack thereof)

Vision should be progressive, not static. Mission is there to serve the vision. When there is no vision to pursue, mission becomes self-serving, and goals become pointless in terms of helping to fulfill a non-existent vision.

"If people can't see what God is doing, they stumble all over themselves; But when they attend to what he reveals, they are most blessed."

~Pro. 29:18 - MSG

RECONCILIATION (On Purpose)

"You know the story of how Adam landed us in the dilemma we're in—first sin, then death, and no one exempt from either sin or death. That sin disturbed relations with God in everything and everyone, but the extent of the disturbance was not clear until God spelled it out in detail to Moses. So death, this huge abyss separating us from God, dominated the landscape from Adam to Moses. Even those who didn't sin precisely as Adam did by disobeying a specific command of God still had to experience this termination of life, this separation from God. But Adam, who got us into this, also

points ahead to the One who will get us out of it. Yet the rescuing gift is not exactly parallel to the death-dealing sin. If one man's sin put crowds of people at the dead-end abyss of separation from God, just think what God's gift poured through one man, Jesus Christ, will do! There's no comparison between that death-dealing sin and this generous, life-giving gift. The verdict on that one sin was the death sentence; the verdict on the many sins that followed was this wonderful life sentence. If death got the upper hand through one man's wrongdoing, can you imagine the breathtaking recovery life makes, sovereign life, in those who grasp with both hands this wildly extravagant life-gift, this grand setting-every-thing-right, that the one man Jesus Christ provides? Here it is in a nutshell: Just as one person did it wrong and got us in all this trouble with sin and death, another person did it right and got us out of it. But more than just getting us out of trouble, he got us into life! One man said no to God and put many people in the wrong; one man said yes to God and put many in the right. All that passing laws against sin did was produce more lawbreakers. But sin didn't, and doesn't, have a chance in competition with the aggressive forgiveness we call grace. When it's sin versus grace, grace wins hands down. All sin can do is threaten us with death, and that's the end of it. Grace, because God is putting everything together again through the Messiah, invites us into life—a life that goes on and on and on, world without end."

~Rom. 5:12-21 - MSG

A SON'S REWARD

Sin entered the world through one man

And death entered the world through sin
In this way all men died
Because all men have sinned

But the gift of God is eternal life
Through Jesus Christ the Lord
Those who yield to do God's will
Receive a son's reward

(W. Berry / See & Say Songs, BMI)

Based on the narrative from Rom. 5:12-21, we find a Biblical explanation of what the plan of reconciliation is and how it's to be outworked in the lives of those who willingly and humbly receive such a grand gift. The harsh implications of sin upon all of humanity is clearly spelled out in that passage. However, the way of restoration and renewal (redemption), are also made evident through the saving grace of God manifested in and through the life of Christ Jesus. The word *reconciliation* isn't stated in the text, but the plan itself is there in seed form. The "ministry of reconciliation" and its unfolding is fully displayed in 2 Cor. 5:18-21. That passage links directly to the Rom. 5:12-21 narrative. In them, there are two key components at work in both passages. One being the "ministry of reconciliation". The other being the role as an "ambassador for Christ."

This chapter, and the one following, address how both aspects link up with our kingdom citizenship as we live out a kingdom life—or lifestyle.

I'm not going to go into lengthy detail as to the meaning and implications of reconciliation. You can do that on your own time, and at your own pace if you choose. What I'll do here is focus in on the main text that I believe deals with the subject at hand. It is presented in 2 Cor. 5:18-21 (NASB) which says,

> *"Now all these things are from God, who reconciled us to Himself through Christ and gave us the ministry of reconciliation, namely, that God was in Christ reconciling the world to Himself, not counting their trespasses against them, and He has committed to us the word of reconciliation. Therefore, we are ambassadors for Christ, as though God were making an appeal through us; we beg you on behalf of Christ, be reconciled to God. He made Him who knew no sin to be sin on our behalf, so that we might become the righteousness of God in Him."*

Here are the target points:

- The plan of Reconciliation was created by the Father, pasted on to the Son, and thereafter imparted to those who are "with Christ in God" (Col. 3:1-3), having been reconciled to the Father through Jesus (see 2 Cor. 5:18).
- The plan of Reconciliation was formulated in eternity. It has been active on earth—in earth-time—since Jesus brought it with Him. But, *it is not time-bound*. It is an eternal principle established to have no end.
- The plan has only one pre-condition for it to become effective in someone's life. It must be accepted (received). In other words, *the entire human race has the *potential to be reconciled through union with Christ Jesus* (see Rom. 10:13). The work to put that in place has already been completed (Jn. 17:4 and 19:30). All that's required for anybody/everybody to secure reconciliation is to take/receive it as their own. There are no other requirements.

No class system issues or exclusions. No race restrictions. No color barriers. No secret code. No nationalistic birthrights to present as documentation, etc. (see 2 Cor. 5:19).

*The *potential* is there for reconciliation to take place. However, everyone will not accept it. Potential means there is a possibility. It does not mean that it has been fulfilled in total. All of humanity will not be saved. That would be universalism, and Christianity is certainly not universalism. God's plan of reconciliation through the redemptive work of Christ is on a person-to-person basis—one redeemed soul at a time.

- Anyone who is serving as an ambassador for Christ by extending the "ministry of reconciliation" to humanity-at-large must do so by placing no restrictions on anyone that is not mentioned in verse 19. If reconciliation is offered with the proviso that *some restrictions may apply*, then that ministry isn't the same as what Jesus imparts to those who follow Him.

The implications of this point are huge within the body of Christ. We are missing this point big time!
One of the keys which explains why all this is taking place is found in Heb. 2:10 which says;

"For it was fitting for Him, for whom are all things, and through whom are all things, in bringing many sons to glory, to perfect the author of their salvation through suffering."

That verse (as I understand it) builds a bridge which extends retroactively back to The Fall. It tells us why man was created (to establish relationship), how that relationship was broken (through the sin of disobedience), who became the agent to reach across the divide through reconciliation (Christ Jesus), and how to accomplish what the Trinity intended to bring to pass from the moment that *"Let us make man in our image"* was uttered. The objective has been, is now, and will always be to *"bring many sons to glory."*

There's a lot to unpack in that verse. So, let's start here.

In a conversation which took place in eternity (outside of earth-time), the Trinity said, *"Let us make man in our image"* (Gen. 1:26). That creative formation wasn't just a visual representation. The image was to be a fully-fashioned likeness, just as God intended. Then, God introduced and framed earth-time to provide a context in which the history of humanity on earth was to take place. The Trinity being as it were, relational, a way, and a place to interact was established. The way was relational and the place was The Garden (see Gen. 2 and 3).

Then, sin entered the world and took up residence in the heart and soul of man when The Fall took place. Relationship was then broken by the self-serving-disobedient-actions of Adam and Eve.

At the moment when that transpired, the Sovereign Creator set in motion a plan—fashioned in eternity before earth-time began—by which relationship(s) between the Trinity and humankind could be restored. That plan was/is reconciliation.

The writer of Hebrews provides us with an overview of how the entire fulfillment was designed to work in Heb. 2:10 which states:

> *"For it was fitting for Him, for whom are all things, and through whom are all things, in bringing many sons to glory, to perfect the author of their salvation through suffering."*

I see in that verse the entire plan of redemption, set within the context of reconciliation. In Wayne-Speak that verse says this:

God (Creator of all there is) had a plan in mind that was of His own making and implementation. So, it was perfect! The plan was for *"bringing many sons (and daughters) to glory."* (addition mine) The unfolding process was to require the sending, and sacrificing of His only Son, Jesus, to earth. Through the suffering, death, burial, and resurrection of Christ, the fulfillment manifested in accordance with God's Divine intention.

If you were to consider the Heb. 2:10 text as a bridge, you could stand on this side of it and look back across it over time. It would extend from our current earth-time all the way back to The Garden and The Fall. That's where the footings were first set in place for its construction. Its expanse covers all of time and history. If you were to walk across it from where it begins, you could look over the side railing and see the unfolding of human history taking place with every step you took.

For me, that verse is monumental in its importance, and overlooked in our consideration of what it tells us in regard to the impartation of God's perfect will for humanity. He wants us with Him, so He designed and then released a way here on earth for us to join Him as kingdom citizens, in heaven, in eternity. And, between now and then, we are to serve in the kingdom of His dear Son. We do that by extending the ministry of reconciliation, as ambassadors for Christ.

I am aware that I've been repeating myself in terms of content. I do so because I believe this subject matter to be so very important to our individual lives as followers of Christ. I also believe it is important for the church-at-large as it relates to our active relevance as living witnesses to humanity. Further, I believe the very root of the fruit that can manifest from gaining a better understanding of such matters is worship—the obedient service of self-sacrifice.

{Selah...pause and ponder}

As I began closing out this chapter, I'll reinforce two things by mentioning them again:
According to 2 Cor. 5:18-21, each/every follower of Christ has two things that they are specifically charged with.

They are given the "ministry of reconciliation" to offer/extend to *everyone* in direct accord with how it was given to us through Jesus from God. That is the job assignment of *every individual Christian.*

The job title of *every individual Christian* is to serve God's kingdom as an ambassador of Christ.

The body of Christ is filled to overflowing with so-called believers who don't have a clue what either of those two points mean or how to apply them to the life of service they say they are offering to the Lord.

Now, begin to process that as the Holy Ghost leads you, remaining open to fresh revelation in that regard.

An Axiom
Revelation leads to Transformation
Transition leads to Impartation

{Selah...pause and ponder}

CHRIST'S FAMILY DNA

"In Christ's family there can be no division into Jew and

non-Jew, slave and free, male and female. Among us you are all equal. That is, we are all in a common relationship with Jesus Christ. Also, since you are Christ's family, then you are Abraham's famous 'descendant,' heirs according to the covenant promises."

~Gal. 3:28 - MSG

"The Messiah has made things up between us so that we're now together on this, both non-Jewish outsiders and Jewish insiders. He tore down the wall we used to keep each other at a distance. He repealed the law code that had become so clogged with fine print and footnotes that it hindered more than it helped. Then he started over. Instead of continuing with two groups of people separated by centuries of animosity and suspicion, he created a new kind of human being, a fresh start for everybody."

~Eph. 2:14, 15 - MSG

That passage offers us yet another example of how the ministry of reconciliation ebbs and flows throughout Scripture. biblically speaking, it's woven in like a golden thread. As such it binds so many of the principles and precepts of God's Word together. I like to think of the fashioning of such a garment in this way:

"It was given to her to clothe herself in fine linen, bright and clean; for the fine linen is the righteous acts of the saints."

~Rev. 19:8

One last verse which expresses our responsibility toward being unified as a *family* in regard to how we sort all this out:

"...work out your own salvation with fear and trembling."
-Phil. 2:12

From today's contemporary perspective theologically, we have a tendency to frame so much of our understanding of kingdom matters in terms of ourselves instead of as a collective part of the body of Christ.

Whereas, if you read chapter two of Philippians in its entirety, you'll perhaps note that verse 12 isn't written as a directive to be applied to a singular individual. Rather, it is addressing a corporate group of believers. They/We are *collectively* being charged with working out their/our belief system (salvation), together.

The validation of our kingdom citizenship, our unity of spirit and purpose, the ministry of reconciliation, and ambassadorship for Christ is a once-and-for-all directive. If we could begin to implement such dynamics, things on the planet could be transformed in profound and powerful ways. We'd be modeling the *"on earth as it is in heaven"* portion of the prayer Jesus gave to His disciples to use as their own. That'd be a process worth promoting, don't ya think? For real!

CHAPTER THREE
AMBASSADORS FOR CHRIST

"Therefore, we are ambassadors for Christ, as though God were making an appeal through us."

~2 Cor. 5:20

SEEING WHAT WE'RE SAYING

The body of Christ has cultivated a culture of language "in the house" that seems to restrict the kingdom of God here on earth, rather than helping to see it expand worldwide throughout human-kind.

Aren't we supposed to be advancing it? According to the Word that's exactly what we're to do.

"Thy kingdom come, Thy will be done, here on earth as it is in heaven."

~Mat. 6:10

Well, how is it in heaven? For one thing, the kingdom continues to grow there, expanding open-ended as souls are converted, and then transferred from the kingdom of darkness to the kingdom of light. So, part of our role is evangelism (i.e. soul winning). If that is a component of our service here on earth, how is it to be done?

There are two clearly-defined aspects from Scripture which answer that question. One is in the last chapter. It is to extend the ministry of reconciliation—our job. The other is to do so as ambassadors for Christ—our job title.

This is what I see that taking place:

Often, we learn to use biblically-based-Scriptural-language without knowing what it means. In other words, we adopt the lingo, with little understanding of exactly how to apply it—based on what the words themselves intend. As a result, we are diminished in our thinking as it relates to the proper context and the fitting application of much of what we *say* we believe. We are like students in school who learn what to say to pass an exam, or get promoted to an upper class, while at the same time having no practical way of putting our language into practice. As a result, we tend to know how to talk the talk, without walking the walk.

What I've just said is essential to how we view and understand ambassadorship. Allow me to develop my postulation with some examples:

We sing, pray, and plead for God's presence to come among us without giving clear consideration to what the word Omnipresent means. My understanding of Omnipresence is that God is everywhere, all the time. Although He may not show up (manifest), He is nonetheless ever-present—if He is in fact Omnipresent. The psalmist tells us that very clearly in Ps. 139:7-12 (MSG) when he states,

> *"Is there any place I can go to avoid your Spirit to be out of your sight? If I climb to the sky, you're there! If I go underground,*

you're there! If I flew on morning's wings to the far western horizon, You'd find me in a minute—you're already there waiting! Then I said to myself, 'Oh, he even sees me in the dark! At night I'm immersed in the light!' It's a fact: darkness isn't dark to you; night and day, darkness and light, they're all the same to you."

I can hear Paul's words echoing what the psalmist says above, with his comment,

"You realize, don't you, that you are the temple of God, and God himself is present in you?"
~1 Cor. 3:16 - MSG

Those words are presented as a question, which is what they are. But, they are also (from my POV) a sort of reminder to those who are *"with God in Christ"* (Col. 3:3). It's as if he is saying that in case we forget where God is, he wants to remind us that even though we don't see Him manifested, or feel Him moving (emotionally), He is nonetheless there.

The issue isn't where God is, why we don't see Him, or what is keeping Him from moving among us. The key word is *realize*. We don't *realize* He's here because we don't own the proper understanding of what Omnipresent means. That seems to be Paul's point. It's mine, too.

A Disclaimer: If you think I'm trying to correct your theology (or anyone else's) you're mistaken. My comments aren't intended as corrective. Rather, they are for the purpose of instruction. I am attempting to provoke you to consider what you know about what you think you know, by giving you examples of the disparity between what we say, and what we think about what we say—in terms of how we speak and apply Scriptural language. This all has to do with ambassadorship. Bear with me, I'm still laying a foundation for that.

Saying that we need God to *show up* in light of what Ps. 139 says is (to me) a clear contradiction in thinking, language-wise. How can we say we need His presence, if His presence is already with us? See what I mean? We aren't thinking about what we're saying, so we don't realize that we are making a request for God to come, when, in fact, He's everywhere all the time. Let me put it to you this way: Where is God not? The answer is that He's not nowhere. Everywhere there is a *where*, He is present.

Again, please remember that my point isn't to address this in terms of right vs. wrong. I'm just trying to point out the disconnect we have in terms of how we use some of our church lingo, without really giving much thought to what we're saying. Let's press on.

We say that part of our responsibility is to help advance God's kingdom here on earth "as it is in heaven." But, when it comes to sorting out what that means and how to put it into practice, we often don't seem to know where to begin. That brings me to the subject I'm addressing in this chapter—ambassadorship.

In the last chapter, I tried to sort out some of what I understand to be the job description of *every* follower of Christ. In the same passage in 2 Cor. 5:18-21, we are given our job title, which is linked directly with our job description. We're given the ministry of reconciliation to carry out as ambassadors for Christ. But, as I've been stating, we use the proper language, but we don't know what it means in order to put it into practice.

If you personally don't know what the phrase, *ambassador for Christ*, means it may be for one of the following reasons:

- You've never taken the time or had the opportunity to learn what an *ambassador* is and how they discharge their roles as such.
- You've not been exposed to anyone who teaches on the subject of *ambassadorship*.
- You don't care because you're distracted, disinterested, or disengaged from the very title you've been given as a gift from God.
- There are lots of other potential reasons. But, you likely get the point already.

Saying we're serving as ambassadors for Christ, without knowing what that service entails, is to a great extent why we aren't seeing reconciliation to Christ Jesus taking place on anywhere near the level that it could/should be among desperate and dying humanity.

Over the last several years, I've come to believe that our lack of understanding in regard to our calling to minister reconciliation, combined with our lack of clarity related to our titled position, has a direct bearing on why the level of influence and significance has so diminished outside the walls of our churches. Simply stated, we don't seem to know why we're here, or what to do while we are.

The fundamental reason for that (as I see it) is a lack of knowledge, understanding, and wisdom. We need to gather the data—that's information. Then we need to process it—that's interpreting with understanding. Thereafter, we can begin to apply the wisdom we've acquired as we're trained to do our jobs, with the title (authority) we've been given.

With that in mind, here are two articles related to how an ambassador is to carry out their service to the nation they represent. They provide some much needed insight as to how such a position is to be understood and undertaken in the discharge of duty. I offer them to you for your personal and corporate consideration. They have helped me in my own quest for clarity. Perhaps they'll help you as well.

10 Essential Qualities of an Effective Ambassador for Christ

Representing Christ today requires three basic skills. First, Christ's ambassadors need the basic *knowledge* necessary for the task. They must know the central message of God's kingdom and something about how to respond to the obstacles they'll encounter on their diplomatic mission.

However, it is not enough for followers of Jesus to have an accurately informed mind. Our knowledge must be tempered with the kind of *wisdom* that makes our message clear and persuasive. This requires the tools of a diplomat, not the weapons of a warrior, tactical skill rather than brute force.

Finally, our *character* can make or break our mission. Knowledge and wisdom are packaged in a person, so to speak. If that person does not embody the virtues of the kingdom he serves, he will undermine his message and handicap his efforts.

These three skills—knowledge, an accurately informed mind; wisdom, an artful method; and character, an attractive manner—play a part in every effective involvement with a nonbeliever. The second skill, tactical wisdom, is the main focus of my book *Tactics*.

If you are an attentive student, in a very short time you will develop the art of maintaining appropriate control—what I call "staying in the driver's seat"—in discussions with others. You will learn how to navigate through the minefields to gain a footing or an advantage in conversations. In short, you will be learning to be a better diplomat—an ambassador for Jesus Christ.

An ambassador is:

Ready. An ambassador is alert for chances to represent Christ and will not back away from a challenge or an opportunity.

Patient. An ambassador won't quarrel, but will listen in order to understand, then with gentleness will seek to respectfully engage those who disagree.

Reasonable. An ambassador has informed convictions (not just feelings), gives reasons, asks questions, aggressively seeks answers, and will not be stumped by the same challenge twice.

Tactical. An ambassador adapts to each unique person and situation, maneuvering with wisdom to challenge bad thinking, presenting the truth in an understandable and compelling way.

Clear. An ambassador is careful with language and will not rely on Christian lingo nor gain unfair advantage by resorting to empty rhetoric.

Fair. An ambassador is sympathetic and understanding toward others and will acknowledge the merits of contrary views.

Honest. An ambassador is careful with the facts and will not misrepresent another's view, overstate his own case, or understate the demands of the gospel.

Humble. An ambassador is provisional in his claims, knowing that his understanding of truth is fallible. He will not press a point beyond what his evidence allows.

Attractive. An ambassador will act with grace, kindness, and good manners. He will not dishonor Christ in his conduct.

Dependent. An ambassador knows that effectiveness requires joining his best efforts with God's power.

—Gregory Koukl,
Tactics: A Game Plan for Discussing Your Christian Convictions,
Zondervan, 2009

An Axiom
Knowledge is Information
Understanding is Interpretation
Wisdom is Application

How to Conduct Ourselves as Ambassadors for Christ

To the members of God's church in Philippi, the apostle Paul writes, "For our citizenship is in heaven" (Philippians 3:20). While some may spiritualize this fact away, Paul's words come across as literal and real to those who understand that God has called us out of this world (John 15:19) and transferred us into His Kingdom (Colossians 1:13).

Having our citizenship in the Kingdom of God by definition makes us aliens in the physical country in which we live. Like ambassadors of a foreign government, we cannot participate in the politics of another country, a practice that would distract us from our real spiritual goal. However, we realize that the apostle Paul has challenged us to be ambassadors for Christ: "Therefore we are ambassadors for Christ, as though God were pleading through us: we implore you on Christ's behalf, be reconciled to God" (II Corinthians 5:20).

Do we have what it takes to be ambassadors of Jesus Christ? Do any of us know what an ambassador is supposed to do, or how an ambassador should behave? Do we know how an ambassador is expected to interface with the various publics with which he comes into contact?

A REAL AMBASSADOR

I met my first ambassador about seventeen years ago in Pasadena, California, when a fellow Ambassador College faculty member introduced me to the Press and Cultural Consulate of Finland, Mr. Jaako Bergquist. I struck up an informal conversation with him, mentioning I had lived and taught in a Finnish community up in Moose Lake, Minnesota. Since the faculty member had previously told Ambassador Bergquist that I hosted a classical music program on KBAC, the college radio station, I also informed him that Jean Sibelius—a Finn—was my favorite composer.

A week later, my colleague and I were invited to a get-together at the consulate's home in Beverly Hills. I had no idea what to expect, but I counted it as an opportunity to learn a little bit more about the diplomatic community. Through this, as well as other later encounters, I gained a better insight on what an ambassador does. Subsequently, I have had several opportunities to talk with Dr. Zion Evrony, the Israeli Consul General to the Southwest Region, when he visited Longview and Tyler, Texas.

A consulate, incidentally, is a branch embassy headed by a Consul General and many junior consuls. The Israeli Consulate for the American Southwest region, for example, is based in Houston. Its service area includes Texas, Louisiana, Arkansas, Oklahoma, and New Mexico. It does not have the same kind of diplomatic immunity as the main embassy in the nation's capital, but it is a real branch of an embassy, carrying on the same business that an embassy does.

Consulates are found in every major city, conducting the business of the countries they represent within the regional spheres of influence of those cities. We might draw a parallel between the embassy of a foreign country and the churches of God (whose real citizenship and headquarters are in heaven). The main embassies of Finland and Israel are located in Washington, DC, but consulates are found in New York City, Chicago, Los Angeles, Houston, and a number of other major metropolitan areas.

We could consider one of God's embassies to be the headquarters of one the churches of God with the leading pastor or evangelist serving as the Chargé d'Affaires or the Consul General. The branch consulates are the individual, outlying congregations with its members serving as junior consuls. Every baptized church member's home could be designated as a branch consulate for the Kingdom of God. Realizing that we are members of God's diplomatic corps, it is important to know how to behave as a diplomat.

The first thing that impressed me at the get-together was the humble and gracious attitude and manner of our host, Jaako Bergquist. Mr. Bergquist assumed the position of a humble servant or steward, looking after the interests of his country, as well as serving and helping people like me to learn more about his country and its culture. For example, when he learned about my classical music radio program, he asked me if I would like to receive some musical recordings. Later that week, I received a package of fifteen long-playing records containing the complete symphonic works of Jean Sibelius. We played these recordings many times over KBAC and KBAU.

Jaako Bergquist was not a glad-handed super-salesman for his country, but more of an accommodating steward practicing what the apostle Paul counsels us to observe in Philippians 2:4: "Let each of you look out not only for his own interests, but also for the interests of others." Accordingly, the Finnish diplomat did not seem to be self-interested in the least, but was always interested in supplying the needs of others, actively esteeming others more than himself (verse 3).

A CULTURAL REPRESENTATIVE

A member of the diplomatic community realizes his extreme vulnerability as a minority member of a majority alien culture. Whether we like it or not, that role fits all of us. In such a position, a diplomat must be circumspect in all his words and activities, careful not to offend his hosts or bring disrepute upon his homeland.

I was amazed at how many of the qualifications of an elder or overseer Paul lists in I Timothy 3:1-7 that Jaako Berquist possessed, including hospitality, the ability to teach, having his home in tip-top order, and exercising temperance and self-control. Like a busy switch engine in the Union Pacific freight yard, the industrious ambassador constantly moved from guest to guest, linking people together with common interests. At one point during the evening, he made sure I became acquainted with the Program Director of KUSC, a classical music station run by the University of Southern California. Later, he introduced to me an elderly couple from Esko, Minnesota, who had lived close to the community where I used to teach.

He made available, but did not push, the culture of Finland, somewhat like the philosophy of the Hershey Chocolate Company, which at one time relied largely on goodwill and word of mouth to advertise its products.

Occasionally, we may be afforded opportunities to assist other church of God groups with a special need. Not long ago, a local minister was somewhat vexed by intruders from other groups attempting to persuade members of his flock about the Nisan 15 Passover. Sabbath.org—one of our church's websites—contains a series of abstracts on sermons that thoroughly examines the subject. After downloading and printing these sermon abstracts, I dropped them off at the local minister's office on my way home from work. I reassured him that I did not want to proselytize or steal sheep, but only wanted to provide resources to help him defend his flock. To what extent he used those documents or how deeply his curiosity was piqued, I do not know, but he expressed a great deal of gratitude for those resources, promising that he would bookmark our site.

Another of our websites, BibleTools.org, provides another non-threatening resource to the greater church of God and the world at large, providing a lavish smorgasbord of truth and choice spiritual meat for those starving for understanding. Just pointing people to these resources can be a diplomatic way of availing others of the culture of the Kingdom of God.

At the Consulate's get-together in Beverly Hills, there were gentle but ubiquitous reminders that we guests were at a Finnish party: abundant Finnish food, Finnish vodka, Finnish artwork, murals and paintings of Finnish lakes and forests—reminding me of northern Minnesota and of northern Wisconsin—Finnish books, and Finnish symphonic and folk music playing over speakers throughout the residence. I became extremely homesick for Suomi or Finland—and I am not even Finnish!

GRACIOUS SPEECH

Besides humility and hospitality, Mr. Bergquist demonstrated diplomacy and wisdom, speaking very circumspectly, carefully considering the consequences of what he said, extremely careful not to injure the feelings of others needlessly. Later, while comparing notes, my colleague mentioned that he never heard Jaako Bergquist or any other member of the diplomatic community let his personal feelings enter the discussion. He merely repeated the official position of his country.

Likewise, we junior consuls of the government of God need to keep our pet opinions to ourselves (or at least qualify them as our own pet opinions). However, we must be knowledgeable of God's Word on any given subject, being ready to give an answer (I Peter 3:15). In addition, our words must model the gracious speech of our Elder Brother, who in John 14:10 says, "The words that I speak to you I do not speak on my own authority; but the Father who dwells in Me does the works."

Without scriptural backing, our own opinions are largely useless hot air. Consequently, as diplomates (sic) of God's government, we must learn to submerge our own feelings, being quick to listen and slow to speak, reflecting Jesus' half-brother's admonition in James 1:19.

Give no offense, either to the Jews or to the Greeks or to the church of God [perhaps during the current scattering the most difficult task of all], just as I also please all men in all things, not seeking my own profit, but the profit of many, that they may be saved. (emphasis added 1 Cor. 10:32, 33 – NASB)

Paul's mentor in diplomatic skills, Jesus Christ, had earlier proclaimed, "Woe to that man by whom the offense comes!" (Matthew 18:7). Some of us have been past masters at creating offenses, being wise as doves and harmless as serpents! As Christ's ambassadors, we must repent of such behavior.

If we want to follow the example of the master diplomat, the apostle Paul, schooled under both Jesus Christ and Gamaliel, we should look at a significant encounter he had with the philosophers at Athens in Acts 17. To begin, Paul paid the Athenians a compliment: "Then Paul stood in the midst of the Areopagus and said, 'Men of Athens, I perceive that in all things you are very religious'" (Acts 17:22).

If we were to read between the lines, Paul might be saying, "You Athenians are to be commended for your devotion to spiritual things." The King James' rendering of "religious" as "superstitious" exposes the latter word as having undergone what linguists call semantic drift. In Shakespeare's day and King James' time, this word did not have the negative connotation as it does now.

From the context of this account, it is plain that the apostle Paul was not, as some theologians like to characterize him, a feisty, wrangling, argumentative hothead. The men of Athens, who vastly outnumbered Paul and loved a good philosophical debate, could have made short work out of any know-it-all smart aleck. The apostle Paul was thus lavish in his compliments.

Throughout his ministry, he frequently resorted to diplomatic language. At one point, he acknowledged a cultural debt both to the Greeks and to barbarians (Romans 1:14). In addition to complimenting strangers, Paul continually sought out similarities he shared between him and other groups. In a conflict in which both the Sadducees and the Pharisees were breathing fire down his neck, Paul masterfully ingratiated himself to the Pharisees, reminding them that he and they shared the same view on the resurrection (Acts 23:6-8). Paul, to the right people, let it be known that he was a Roman citizen (Acts 16:37-39; 22:25-29).

COMMON GROUND

We also need to find common ground, not only with people in the other groups of the church of God, but with the world at large, emphasizing (like mountains) the things we agree upon and de-emphasizing (like molehills) the things we disagree upon.

In the process of finding common ground, we dare not compromise our core values or syncretize them with the world. We should instead practice more of what the late church of God minister, Sherwin McMichael, counseled, "You don't have to tell all you know." Oftentimes, keeping our traps shut is the most diplomatic behavior of all (Ecclesiastes 3:7; Lamentations 3:28-29; Amos 5:13).

In Acts 17:23, the apostle Paul deliberately builds a

bridge of common understanding and similarity, referring to something the Athenians already understood:

For as I was passing through and considering the objects of your worship, I even found an altar with this inscription: TO THE UNKNOWN GOD. Therefore, the one whom you worship without knowing [a more proper rendering than "ignorantly," another word that has also undergone semantic drift] Him I proclaim to you."

Later, in verse 28, Paul again seeks common ground by quoting from their own literature: "For in Him we live and move and have our being, as also some of your own poets have said, 'For we are also His offspring.'"

The important thing to remember is that the apostle Paul started at the Athenians' current level of understanding, continually finding commonalities between himself and his audience upon which to build mutual understanding and foster growth. An ambassador skillfully demonstrates how his country and another's country share similar interests. As the late Rabbi Meir Kahane pointed out, an alliance is not so much built on friendship as on common interests.

To summarize, in successful diplomatic negotiating, points we agree upon must be stressed and any disagreements must be de-emphasized. An ambassador should never be a pushy salesman or a glad-handed public relations man. Whatever his rank in the diplomatic community, Ambassador, Consul General, Chargé d'Affaires, junior consul, envoy, or diplomat, he has the following characteristics:

1. He is a representative of another culture, another way of life.

2. In this capacity, he does not give his own opinions, but advances the positions of his home country.

3. He functions as a servant or steward, representing his country faithfully.

4. As such, he practices hospitality, courtesy, and graciousness.

Proverbs 13:17 reads, "A wicked messenger falls into trouble, but a faithful ambassador brings health." As faithful ambassadors of Christ, we ought to bring health, refreshment, and comfort to the people with whom we come into contact.

—David F. Maas
Forerunner, January 2004 (used by permission)

How can someone become an ambassador without knowing as much as possible about the country/nation they are charged with representing? The answer is a simple one—they can't. Or, if they attempt to do so, they will do a poor job of it.

I'll point out a few personal observation to help bring this topic into sharper focus:

1. An ambassador doesn't apply for their position. They are appointed.
2. Even if they are qualified to serve (based on some aspects of past experiences or giftings) they will still have a considerable amount of on-the-job-training to do once they relocate to their assigned station of service.
3. They are not responsible for trying to convert the citizens of the nation they are sent to.
4. They are stationed in a foreign land as representatives of their home nation. By modeling the principles, precepts,

cultural distinctions, and core values of their nation, through their example, citizens of the nation they've been sent to can then begin to gain insight into the ambassador's homeland.
5. While in service, an ambassador is to follow the protocol of their homeland, while at the same time showing respect and consideration for the people and the nation where they've been assigned to live until their tour of duty is finished.
6. While in service, they do not attempt to become like the nationals in the country they've been assigned to reside in. Rather, they are to maintain their own citizenship as if they were still living in their homeland.

They are in essence to live *"...in the world, but not of it"* (Jn. 17:14, 15).

If someone takes on the role of an ambassador for Christ with the intention of representing themselves, their own agendas, or the temporal values of the country they were born in (nationalization), they are not going to be able to function in the manner to which they have been called to serve. The job assignment is to always bear in mind that every aspect of representation is to be based on knowing how to apply the protocols, principles, and precepts found in their resource manual—the Bible.

There is a difference between representing a foreign government as its ambassador and attempting to require others (in their own nation) to adhere to the ways of the government of the one we are serving. An ambassador is to uphold their own government, not try to force others to conform to a way of life which they no little to nothing about.

I view the process that I'm addressing as living as a witness, as opposed to witnessing. Witnessing as an ambassador is for me, a misnomer. An ambassador *is* a witness. They are not called to *do* witnessing. They are, in fact, serving *as* a witness. Witnesses give testimony by what they say and do. Wherever they are, they are there as witnesses. Even if they never open their mouths—their very presence speaks to who they are and why they're there.

If that seems like I'm playing fast and loose with the language as you understand the term, *witness*, perhaps you could reconsider Acts 1:8 which says,

> *"...but you will receive power when the Holy Spirit has come upon you; and you shall be My witnesses both in Jerusalem, and in all Judea and Samaria, and even to the remotest part of the earth."*
>
> (Emphasis mine)

To me, that reads pretty much like a commissioning proclamation to be considered and applied in order to take up an assignment as an ambassador for Christ.

Come with me a little further down this pathway.

Look at the dynamic which unfolds in Ex. 33:12-16. There is a scenario there that is worth revisiting.

> *"Moses said to God, 'Look, you tell me, "Lead this people," but you don't let me know whom you're going to send with me. You tell me, "I know you well and you are special to me." If I am so special to you, let me in on your plans. That way, I will continue being special to you. Don't forget, this is your people, your responsibility.' God said, 'My presence will go*

with you. I'll see the journey to the end.' Moses said, 'If your presence doesn't take the lead here, call this trip off right now. How else will it be known that you're with me in this, with me and your people? Are you traveling with us or not? How else will we know that we're special, I and your people, among all other people on this planet Earth?'"

~Ex. 33:12-16 – MSG (Emphasis mine)

I could spend a very long time unpacking all that's in the passage above. But, as it relates to ambassadorship, I'm going to focus on the last sentence. I see it as a foundational text regarding living as a witness, evangelism, ambassadorship, and kingdom expansion.

The KJV translates that sentence as follows:

"...so shall we be separated, I and thy people, from all the people that are upon the face of the earth."

The word *separated* means to distinguish; to put as different; to show as marvelous; to set apart, serve, or make wonderful.

The uniqueness that Moses is requesting from Jehovah is based on God's presence going with him and the rest of the wilderness wanderers into areas where those they will know nothing about who they are or why they function as they do. So, in a real sense, Moses is speaking as a prototype representative of ambassadorship. He's been called. He's being sent. He needs covering over his life in order to serve in an authentic manner. He views the living presence of God as the singular component necessary in order to be recognized as different, other, distinguished by those he will come in contact with.

> "*Even now, behold, my witness is in heaven, and he who testifies for me is on high.*"
> ~Job 16:19 - ESV

Now, go with me back to Acts 1:8:

> "*...but you will receive power when the Holy Spirit has come upon you; and you shall be* My *witnesses both in Jerusalem, and in all Judea and Samaria, and even to the remotest part of the earth.*"
> (Emphasis mine)

Re-examine the language.

The contemporary church has shifted the emphasis of that verse so that it focuses on power. But, that isn't where the focus should be. The text says that power will come when (*after*) the Holy Spirit has come. The Holy Spirit is *the* living and active Presence of God. Therefore, power should be understood as a by-product of Presence. If that's correct, then what is the power which comes after Presence there for? The back portion tells us: The empowerment is to *become* witnesses (not to do witnessing). And, where is that to take place? "*... Jerusalem, Judea, Samaria, and the remotest parts of the earth.*" That dear reader, as I see it, is a charge extended to ALL believers to serve as ambassadors for Christ as it is presented to those who consider themselves to be citizens of God's kingdom. That charge is spelled our clearly in 2 Cor. 5:18-21.

Unless and until we begin to accept and live out our job description (ministers of reconciliation) in the authority of our job title (ambassadors for Christ), we will never fully realize the mandate of Acts 1:8. Nor will we be active participants in walking in and serving out of the prayer fulfillment that Moses made in Ex. 33.

Beloved, we have our work cut out for us.

CHAPTER FOUR
CHANNELS OF GRACE

THEOLOGY DEFINED: The study of religious faith, practice, and experience; the study of God and of God's relation to the world.

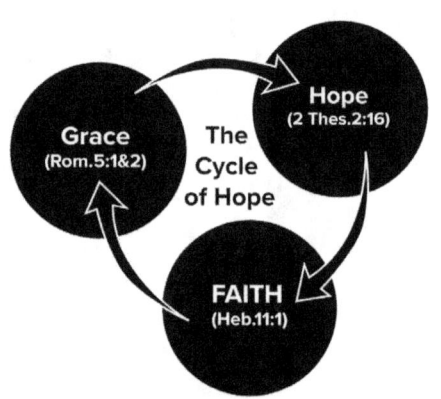

"...to all who are beloved...called as saints: Grace to you and peace from God our Father and the Lord Jesus Christ."
~Rom. 1:7

"...love the Lord with all your heart, soul, *mind, and strength"
~Mt. 12:30

> "...*loving Him with all passion and *intelligence and energy...*"
> ~Mt. 12:30 - MSG

*Mind/Intelligence: Deep thought; the faculty (of mind or disposition); to exercise the imagination; to gain understanding.

What follows in this chapter is a teaching the Holy Ghost birthed in me which I've titled, "The Cycle Of Hope." Working through it will perhaps require some rethinking on your part in regard to what you know about three specific components of your spiritual walk. They are hope, faith, and grace. Each of those aspects of our spirituality are of major importance as they relate to our individual and corporate theology.

Here's the background for how this teaching unfolded.

Over the last few years, I began to notice that the subject of stress-related issues (anxiety, depression, suicide, etc.), were each receiving lots of media coverage through articles, books, social media, and public discourse in general. The rate of increase in each of those areas seems to be moving across multiple generations, and effecting social and cultural groupings at an alarming pace.

Consider this excerpt from an article in the New York Times published in January of 2018 by Ceylan Yeginsu.

> LONDON—Since Britain voted to leave the European Union more than a year ago, Europeans have mockingly said that the decision will result in an isolated, lonely island nation.
>
> But Britain, in fact, already has a serious problem with loneliness, research has found. More than nine million people in the country often or always feel lonely, according

to a 2017 report published by the Jo Cox Commission on Loneliness.

The issue prompted Prime Minister Theresa May on Wednesday to appoint a minister for loneliness.

"For far too many people, loneliness is the sad reality of modern life," Mrs. May said in a statement. I want to confront this challenge for our society and for all of us to take action to address the loneliness endured by the elderly, by carriers, by those who have lost loved ones—and by people who have no one to talk to or share their thoughts and experiences with."

A former United States surgeon general, Dr. Vivek Murthy, wrote an article for the Harvard Business Review last year arguing that loneliness needed addressing in the workplace. It can be associated, he wrote, "with a greater risk of cardiovascular disease, dementia, depression and anxiety."

…In parallel, the Office for National Statistics would help to establish a method of measuring loneliness, and a fund would be set up to help the government and charities to develop a wider strategy to identify opportunities to tackle the problem.

…Government research has found that about 200,000 older people in Britain had not had a conversation with a friend or relative in more than a month.

Based on that research, a new position was established in the government in the U.K. identified as the Minister of Loneliness.

"Ah, look at all the lonely people. Where do they all come from?"

~P. McCartney

There are a number of reports and research papers which I could draw from to address my comments. The percentages and stats would certainly be staggering to considered. But, to realize that a world government has created an official position to deal with the pervasive issue of loneliness on a national level is, to me, an astounding and alarming course of action.

When I became aware of what had taken place in the U.K., I began to give even more prayerful thought to the subject than I had already over the last several years. I saw a link between loneliness and a lack of faith—at least that's what happened on the front end.

However, as I continued to pray and ponder, the subject of hope, or the lack thereof, began to stir in my spirit as well, in a way which drew me back to the Scriptures. That's how my comments to follow came to be. Then, ironically, today as I was working on this chapter a new report from the American Psychological Association was released. Here's a portion of what it says:

GEN Z MORE LIKELY THAN OTHER GENERATIONS TO REPORT FAIR OR POOR MENTAL HEALTH.

Headline issues, from immigration to sexual assault, are causing significant stress among members of Generation Z—those between ages 15 and 21—with mass shootings topping the list of stressful current events, according to the American Psychological Association's report, "Stress in America™: Generation Z" released today.

Specifically, 75 percent of Gen Z members said that mass shootings are a significant source of stress, according to the survey, which was conducted online by The Harris

Poll on behalf of APA in July and August 2018 among 3,458 adults and 300 15–17-year-olds.

Gen Z members are also more stressed than adults overall about other issues in the news, such as the separation and deportation of immigrant and migrant families (57 percent of Gen Z vs. 45 percent of all adults reported the issue is a significant source of stress) and sexual harassment and assault reports (53 percent vs. 39 percent).

America's youngest generation is also significantly more likely (27 percent) than other generations, including Millennials (15 percent) and Gen Xers (13 percent), to report their mental health as fair or poor, the survey found. They are also more likely (37 percent), along with Millennials (35 percent), to report they have received treatment or therapy from a mental health professional, compared with 26 percent of Gen Xers, 22 percent of baby boomers and 15 percent of older adults.

Americans increasingly stressed about the future of the nation

More than 6 in 10 Americans (62 percent) reported that the current political climate is a significant stressor, and more than two-thirds (69 percent) reported that the nation's future causes them stress. This was a significant increase from those who said the same in 2017 (63 percent). Most Americans (61 percent) also disagreed that the country is on a path to being stronger than ever. Because of their concern for the state of the nation, nearly half of Americans (45 percent) said they feel more compelled to volunteer or support causes they value.

Another key finding was that nearly one-quarter (24

percent) of adults identified discrimination as a significant source of stress, the highest percentage since this was first included in the survey in 2015. In 2018, black adults (46 percent) and Hispanic adults (36 percent) reported discrimination as a significant source of stress, compared with 14 percent of white adults.

"Why are you in despair, O my soul, and disturbed within me? Hope in God, because I will again praise him, for the salvation of his presence."

~Ps. 42:5 - LEB

THE SOLID ROCK

My hope is built on nothing less,
than Jesus' blood and righteousness
I dare not trust the sweetest frame,
but wholly lean on Jesus' name

When darkness veils His lovely face,
I rest on His unchanging grace
In every high and stormy gale,
my anchor holds within the veil

His oath, His covenant, His blood,
support me in the whelming flood
When all around my soul gives way,
He then is all my hope and stay

When He shall come with trumpet sound,
oh, may I then in Him be found
Dressed in His righteousness alone,
faultless to stand before the throne
Refrain:

On Christ, the solid Rock, I stand
All other ground is sinking sand,
All other ground is sinking sand

~Edward Mote - Circa 1834

FAITH IN MOTION

"I would have despaired unless I had believed that I would see the goodness of the LORD In the land of the living."

~Ps. 27:13

My studies deepened by thinking that the entire subject of stress-related issues which are increasing all over the world is rooted in a lack of faith. Which, in turn, led me back to the well-known, considered, and quoted verse which defines faith biblically for most of the followers of Christ.

"Faith is the substance of things hoped for, the evidence of things not seen."

~Heb. 11:1

As I ponder that text, I started to see it from a different perspective than I had in times past. I noticed that verse tells us what faith is. It also tells us where it comes from. It does not, however, tell us what faith does. I'll get to that later.

For now, I'll begin by unpacking the Heb. 11:1 text, and in doing so I'll present what I've seen in the process of my postulating.

According to the Scriptural definition in Heb. 11:1, faith is the substance of things hoped for, and the evidence of things not seen (or readily available). That tells us what faith is. It also tells us where the substance and the evidence comes from

—hope. Therefore, without hope there is no faith which can manifest in either a tangible substance or in an evidential form. Said another way, no hope, no faith. Or, little hope, little faith. Continuing along that line of reasoning (based on Scripture), big hope, big faith.

Starting from here, I think it'd be a good idea for you to prepare to readjust your perspective regarding how you consider the topic of faith:

Over the last few generations, the church-at-large has allowed the subject of faith to become a huge topic of consideration and influence within the body of Christ throughout the world. The teaching, preaching, research, and commentary focused on faith has been enormous.

To say that faith has become a major topic of our collective contemporary theology would likely be a point of agreement for any group of believers. That's what the so-called "faith movement" or "faith camp" is all about. However, our focus on faith has, in a sense, served to separate it from the definition that the writer of Hebrews has provided us. That separation, in turn, has allowed faith to become free-standing, or if you will, independent.

However, faith is not an independent subject. It is inter-dependent. Why? Because it only exist as an outgrowth of hope. It is the substance, the evidence, the manifestation of hope in the life of a Christian. What I'm saying is that faith only shows up to then accomplish what it was designed to do, when it has been created/birthed directly out of hope.

When a believer says that their faith seems to have run dry, or that they've lost their faith, their focus is on the wrong thing. When faith is diminished, running low, or lost altogether, the real issues isn't a lack of faith, it's a loss of hope.

As important as faith is in the lives of followers of Christ, it can only (or should only) reach such a high level of importance when it is understood to be a direct result of hope.

When the Word tells us that, *"without faith it is impossible to please God"* (Heb. 11:6), the text is making a sound theological statement. It is telling us that faith is essential to our service for God and His kingdom. But, at the same time, it is also making the assumption that the faith required to please God is first and foremost resident in a believer as a direct result of hope already in place and active in their life. Because if hope isn't present, then faith won't be either. They are interdependently linked.

If we allow our considerations of faith to function in an independent and free-standing fashion, we are focusing on the result of it, not the source of it—which is hope.

HOPE AS AN ENERGIZER

> *"We give thanks to God and the Father of our Lord Jesus Christ, praying always for you. For we heard of your faith in Christ Jesus and your love for all the saints, because of the hope which is laid up for you in heaven, of which you have already heard in the word of the truth of the gospel, which has come to you, as it has in all the world, and brings forth fruit, as it has also in you, since the day you heard it and knew the grace of God in truth."*
>
> ~Col. 1:3-6 - MEV

According to Heb. 11:1, we know what faith is, the substance of things hoped for. We also know where it comes from—hope. Here's what it does.

Faith defined: A way of walking, moving, and living. Having to do with motion.

Think of hope as the accelerator pedal in an automobile. The pedal provides a way for the vehicle to move in any desired/required direction.

> "Take me riding in the car, car;
> take me riding in the car, car;
> take you riding in the car, car;
> I'll take you riding in my car."
>
> ~Woodie Guthrie

In order for the accelerator to propel the vehicle into movement, it must have some sort of fuel source from which to draw its propellant (its energy). It does not, cannot, create its own fuel. It draws its dynamic movement from the fuel itself. The fuel in the tank is what provides the accelerant that the pedal requires to operate properly. If there is little fuel in the tank, the vehicle won't go very far. It may start out well enough, but before long, it will sputter to a stand-still, and stop altogether, due to a lack of fuel.

Keeping with that example, consider the accelerator pedal a hope pedal. Now, consider the fuel to consist of grace. A full tank of grace, will enable the hope pedal to create momentum for the auto to become mobilized by faith. And, there ya go!

Stay with me along this current course for a while longer. I'm going to address where hope comes from and how to get it, shortly.

Paul provides us with a couple of clear vantage points from which to view hope.

Hope defined: Confident expectation or anticipation.

"If we have hope in Christ in this life only, *we are of all men most to be pitied."*
~1 Cor. 15:19 (Emphasis mine)

"If all we get out of Christ is a little inspiration for a few short years, *we're a pretty sorry lot."*
~1 Cor. 15:19 - MSG (Emphasis mine)

When Paul speaks of having hope *"in this life only,"* he is not implying that hope is something available to just believers. His comment is saying that hope *can* be based only in this life, but that way provides only a limited understanding and use of it. When appropriated that way, hope becomes a type of generic resource that is available to any human being—based on who or what they choose to place their hope upon.

In other words, there is a form of temporal hope, as well as an eternal hope. He goes on to say that if the *only* hope we have is based on how it applies to living life on earth, there is a problem with it. The problem being that *"we are of all men most to be pitied."*

Said another way, earth bound hope is a pitiful way to live. Many people do, including Christians. In Titus 2:11-13, he goes on to say

"For the grace of God has appeared (past tense), *bringing salvation to all men* (past tense—See 2 Cor. 5:18-21), *instructing us to deny ungodliness and worldly desires* and *to live sensibly, righteously and godly in the present age, looking for the* blessed hope *and the appearing of the glory of our great God and Savior, Christ Jesus..."*
(Emphasis & addition mine)

Dealing with the last half of that verse first, we are told that we, as followers of Christ, are to *"live sensibly, righteously and godly in the present age."* While doing that, we are to be *"looking for the blessed hope and the appearing of the glory of our great God and Savior, Christ Jesus."*

Here he is making a distinction between worldly/temporal hope, and the hope which is "blessed"—found in Christ. Bear that in mind related to what's coming next on our sojourn.

SOURCING HOPE

"God our Father has given us (past tense) *eternal comfort and good hope by grace."*
~2 Thess. 2:16 (Addition mine)

The verse above tells us where the hope we have comes from. The verse below reinforces that.

"Therefore, prepare your minds for action, keep sober in spirit, fix your hope completely on grace…*"*
~1 Peter 1:13 (Emphasis mine)

Let's review:

1. Faith appears in a life when hope is resident inside.
2. Hope, which is either temporal or eternal, comes from God who gives eternal comfort and good hope by grace.

If those two points are biblically sound, which I believe they are, the question to follow is this: Where does grace come from, which in turn releases hope, which then manifests as faith?

Here's the Scriptural answer:

> "...let us draw near with confidence to the throne of grace, so that we may receive mercy and find grace to help in time of need."
>
> ~Heb. 4:16

I have a working definition of grace that I'd like you to consider as we continue our road trip:

Grace is the unmerited favor of God's empowering presence, enabling me to be who He created me to be, so I can do what He calls me to do.

The grace of God flows from His throne of grace. It is the filling station where we receive what we need of it for our daily journey. Once we've refueled our tank with grace, we can then press down on our hope pedal. Then we're on our way again into a new day, filled with new mercies and divine destiny.

> "The path of the righteous is like the light of dawn, that shines brighter and brighter until the full day."
>
> ~Pro. 4:18

As we journey on, our grace tank will begin to be drained by the distance we're covering. That being the case, we will need to return to the filling station (the throne of grace) in order to refuel. Faith makes that possible.

Romans 5:1 says in part,

> "...faith introduces us to grace."

"By entering through faith into what God has always wanted to do for us—set us right with him, make us fit for him—we have it all together with God because of our Master Jesus. And that's not all: We throw open our doors to God and discover at the same moment that he has already thrown open his door to us. We find ourselves standing where we always hoped we might stand—out in the wide open spaces of God's grace and glory, standing tall and shouting our praise."
~Rom. 5:1, 2 - MSG

Bear in mind that there is a cost involved every time you need a fill up. Biblical grace is not cheap.

"Cheap grace is the grace we bestow on ourselves. Cheap grace is the preaching of forgiveness without requiring repentance, baptism without church discipline, Communion without confession...Cheap grace is grace without discipleship, grace without the cross, grace without Jesus Christ, living and incarnate."
~Dietrich Bonhoeffer

For further consideration see Rom. 6 and note verses 12-19 (MSG).

"That means you must not give sin a vote in the way you conduct your lives. Don't give it the time of day. Don't even run little errands that are connected with that old way of life. Throw yourselves wholeheartedly and full-time—remember, you've been raised from the dead!—into God's way of doing things. Sin can't tell you how to live. After all, you're not living under that old tyranny any longer. You're living in

the freedom of God. So, since we're out from under the old tyranny, does that mean we can live any old way we want? Since we're free in the freedom of God, can we do anything that comes to mind? Hardly. You know well enough from your own experience that there are some acts of so-called freedom that destroy freedom. Offer yourselves to sin, for instance, and it's your last free act. But offer yourselves to the ways of God and the freedom never quits. All your lives you've let sin tell you what to do. But thank God you've started listening to a new master, one whose commands set you free to live openly in his freedom! I'm using this freedom language because it's easy to picture. You can readily recall, can't you, how at one time the more you did just what you felt like doing—not caring about others, not caring about God—the worse your life became and the less freedom you had? And how much different is it now as you live in God's freedom, your lives healed and expansive in holiness?"

The Dynamics of the Cycle of Hope

Hope flows out of grace (2 Thess. 2:16).
Renewed and Increased hope manifests as faith (Heb. 11:1).
Faith (in turn) introduces us to grace (Rom. 5:1 and 2).
And the cycle continues.

While working on this section, I came across a short video from Pastor John Piper. He seems to have used similar GPS coordinates traveling along the same highway that I find myself on.

As I was in the final stage of drafting this manuscript, this found its way to me. I'll just pass it along since it speaks to the subject I've been addressing in this chapter—hope, or the lack thereof.

THE SO-CALLED "Death of Despair"

WHY AMERICANS ARE DYING YOUNGER AND YOUNGER
By John Stonestreet with Roberto Rivera

Years ago, Chuck Colson asked, "Where is the hope?" Too many Americans today have no answer, and it's showing.

These deaths, along with alcohol-related deaths, have been dubbed "deaths of despair" by researchers Anne Case and Angus Deaton.

The "despair" referred to by Case and Deaton is largely economic, resulting from diminished job prospects and other personal disappointments. As Case put it, "Your family life has fallen apart, you don't know your kids anymore, all the things you expected when you started out your life just haven't happened at all."

As a result, people, usually but not always men, turn to alcohol and drugs to ease their pain. An increasing number take their own lives.

Certainly, Case and Deaton's explanation is partially true. But it doesn't explain the 30-percent rise in suicide rates among 15-to-24 year-olds, who haven't experienced these kinds of disappointments. Nor does material deprivation explain why the suicide rate among African Americans and Hispanics is only about a third that of white Americans despite being, on average, poorer.

Something else is going on. And it's related to the word "despair."

Chuck Colson and his friend Richard John Neuhaus used to remind people that despair is a sin. Now if you define "despair" as extreme sorrow or grief, then calling it a sin seems cruel and unfeeling.

But that's not really what despair is. In the Christian view, despair is the opposite of hope. Thomas Aquinas wrote that despair "is due to a man's failure to hope that he will share in the goodness of God." For Aquinas, despair was more dangerous than even unbelief or hatred of God because "by hope we are called back from evils and induced to strive for what is good, and if hope is lost, men fall headlong into vices, and are taken away from good works."

For Aquinas, "nothing is more execrable than despair. For he who despairs loses his constancy in the daily labors of this life, and what is worse, loses his constancy in the endeavor of faith." As the sixth-century theologian Isidore of Seville put it, "to commit a crime is death to the soul; but to despair is to descend into hell."

If there's a better word than "Hell" to describe the despair we are seeing in so many American communities, I'm not aware of it.

Still the question remains, "What is the source of this despair?" The answer lies in Aquinas' words "share in the goodness of God." Put simply, Americans place their hope in the wrong thing.

I'm not only referring to those who kill themselves, whether deliberately or indirectly. They're merely the most vulnerable victims of a worldview that has us, in Isaiah's words, spending money on that which is not bread, and working for what doesn't satisfy.

Their disappointment is more keenly felt than ours, but make no mistake, the expectations our culture imposes on us will ultimately end in death. If not physical death, spiritual death. We're told to seek satisfaction from things that cannot ultimately satisfy us, such as sex, stuff, and self.

The results are what Aquinas would have predicted: a headlong fall into vice and away from seeking to do good. The most vulnerable among us wind up paying the ultimate price.

But to know Christ and His resurrection is to know hope. May we never hide that in a culture that needs it so desperately.

Copyright 2019 by the Colson Center for Christian Worldview. Reprinted from BreakPoint.org with permission.

"If we have hope in Christ in this life only, we are of all men most to be pitied."

~1 Cor. 15:19

The Message Bible says;

"If all we get out of Christ is a little inspiration for a few short years, we're a pretty sorry lot."

{Selah...pause and ponder}

If the "cycle of hope" breaks down, this is what can happen:

To the degree that we lose hope, we lose our faith as well. Since faith is the manifestation of hope (Heb. 11:1), it can only be present if our hope is firmly in place. However, there is a potential loss that may be much greater than that of diminished hope and faith following. When we no longer have proper access to fresh and free-flowing grace, our lives can easily become parched, barren and dry. Once our ability to appropriate grace for ourselves becomes restricted—due to a lack of hope—then our entrance before the throne of grace becomes harder to find due to our lack of faith (Rom. 5:1, 2).

Should that take place, two tragically sad losses occur. First, we can no longer secure grace for ourselves, which is a sorrowful situation indeed. Secondly, we are then limited in regard to acquiring grace to impart to others in their time(s) of need (Heb. 4:16). Thereby restricting our personal ability to serve as channels of grace.

Our salvation remains active and the process of sanctification continues. However, the grace we need to accomplish what we've been created to be, so we can do what we're called to do becomes inconsistent, incomplete, and ineffective for ourselves and for the others we are to extend fresh grace to.

The challenge as I see it, is summed up in a passage I've already mention in this chapter. What it says is so important to the concept of receiving and releasing grace that it bears repeating. Note please that I've added some personal adjustments in order to help focus in on key points in the text.

> *"For the grace of God* has appeared (past tense—that's the so called "first work of grace"), *bringing salvation* to all men (past tense—that's the "ministry of reconciliation" - See 2 Cor. 5:18-21), *instructing us* to deny ungodliness and worldly desires and to live sensibly, righteously and godly in the present age, looking for the Blessed Hope *and the appearing of the glory of our great God and Savior, Christ Jesus, who gave Himself for us to redeem us from every*

lawless deed, and to purify for Himself a people for His own possession, zealous for good deeds."
~Titus 2:11-14 (Emphasis & addition mine)

OUR PLACE IN THE PIPELINE

"Serve one another with the particular gifts God has given each of you, as faithful dispensers of the magnificently varied grace of God."
~1 Peter 4:10 - (Phillips)

The channel of grace flows in two distinct ways. First of all, its origin and its release come directly from God's throne of grace. Some theologians understand that to be the so-called "first work of grace." It flows directly into the lives of those who accept Christ Jesus as their Lord, and Savior. It is, in a very real sense, part of the package of redemption—freely given as a gift from the Father to those who are converted by faith.

"By grace you have been saved, through faith; and that not of yourselves, it is a gift from God; not as a result of works, so that no one may boast."
~Eph. 2:8a

There is nothing a person has to do in order to receive it, except to receive it. Pure and simple. No other arrangements or requirements are necessary in order to partake of such an overwhelming gift!

The other channel flows from the same place—God's throne of grace. However, it is acquired in an entirely different way. That approach is referred to by some theologians as the so-called "second work of grace." The way it is received and manifested is through the action(s) of those who are in Christ. According to Heb. 4:16, believers are to;

"...draw near with *confidence to the throne of grace, so that we may receive mercy and find grace to help in time of need."

*The KJV uses the word *boldly* instead of *confidence*. It means with all outspokenness, i.e. frankness, bluntness, assurance, confidence. That is to say in a matter-of-fact way. We are not to go before the throne of grace and make a timid request for fresh, daily grace. We are to be passion-filled in knowing that we need it, and that it is available for those who will appropriate it. It's as if God were saying, "If you want it, it's here, come and get it."

I could be way off course here, but I think that most of us don't approach the subject of grace, or the acquisition of it in that manner. That's certainly something worth pondering.

This second channel uses our very lives as the conduit through which grace flows. It is first imparted to us, and then it flows through us. Here's how that works:

Hebrews 4:16 states clearly that we can *"find grace to help in time of need."* That is referring to us in our time(s) of need. But, the verse doesn't limit or exclude grace from being appropriated by us to help others in[their time(s) of need. All that's required for that to take place is two things in specific:

1. Go boldly before God's grace throne to request grace for ourselves.
2. While we're there, make a request for an increased portion of grace which the Spirit gives us in order to pass it along

to others as they may need it in their time(s) of need.

When we do that, we become not only the recipients of grace for ourselves. We also become tributaries of free-flowing grace that can be poured into the lives of those who need it. Such actions as that serve to inter-link us to the ministry of reconciliation as well as the ambassadorship for Christ spoken of in 2 Cor. 5:18-21, which I've already addressed in the previous two chapters. I so hope you're begging to see the connection here. These connect points provide us with pathways which can us lead into a broader and deeper understanding of our citizenship in the kingdom of God. Which in turn, helps to develop kingdom life in those who are followers of Christ.

All of this is part of the process of spiritual formation which every follower of Christ is called to. Sanctification is meant to take us from where we were when we were redeemed by the saving grace of God, on to fruit bearing and maturity for the glory and honor of the Father, Son, and Holy Ghost. If you need a Biblical basis for what I'm saying here, apply these two passages:

> *"I am the Vine, you are the branches. When you're joined with me and I with you, the relation intimate and organic, the harvest is sure to be abundant. Separated, you can't produce a thing. Anyone who separates from me is deadwood, gathered up and thrown on the bonfire. But if you make yourselves at home with me and my words are at home in you, you can be sure that whatever you ask will be listened to and acted upon. This is how my Father shows who he is—when you produce grapes, when you mature as my disciples."*
>
> ~Jn. 15:6-8 - MSG

> *"He handed out gifts above and below, filled heaven with his gifts, filled earth with his gifts. He handed out gifts of apostle, prophet, evangelist, and pastor-teacher to train Christ's followers in skilled servant work, working within Christ's body, the church, until we're all moving rhythmically and easily with each other, efficient and graceful in response to God's Son, fully mature adults, fully developed within and without, fully alive like Christ.*
> *No prolonged infancies among us, please. We'll not tolerate babes in the woods, small children who are an easy mark for impostors. God wants us to grow up, to know the whole truth and tell it in love—like Christ in everything. We take our lead from Christ, who is the source of everything we do. He keeps us in step with each other.*
> *His very breath and blood flow through us, nourishing us so that we will grow up healthy in God, robust in love."*
>
> ~Eph. 4:10-16 - MSG

My intention here is not to attempt in any way to diminish the importance of faith in the lives of believers. It is one of the most foundational aspects of how we walk out our spiritual beliefs—our core values.

I'm trying to offer a perspective about it that could enable us to refocus how we see it in relationship to how it's presented in Scripture.

Faith would not exist if there were no hope. And hope is present as it flows out of grace. Thereafter, the faith that is resident in our lives is there to accomplish several things—far more than I will attempt to address here. However, one of those key things faith does is to introduce us to grace as part of a cycle. That cycle looks like this:

**Hope to Faith
Faith to Grace
Grace to Hope**

Each chapter topic in this book can be seen, understood, and appropriated directly from that cycle. Here's how.

By grace we are saved through faith (Eph. 2:8). That provides a way of entering into God's kingdom as citizens based on our personal confession of faith (Rom. 10:9). We are then hidden with Christ in God (Col. 3:3). Thereafter, the redeeming work of Christ Jesus in the lives of those who accept Him as Lord and Savior, begins its work of restoration and renewal (1 Thess. 4:3). That means that what the Father imparted to the Son becomes the very core of how we are to serve in the kingdom (2 Cor. 5:18-21).

That service has many different components to it, but there are two in specific which become part of the charge given to those who are followers of Christ. Those two aspects of our salvation package are:

1. The ministry of reconciliation (our job description)
2. The ambassadorship for Christ (our job title)

Both of those responsibilities are imparted to us through grace which I have defined as: The unmerited favor of God's empowering presence, enabling me to be who He created me to be, so I can do what He calls me to do.

The unmerited favor is His grace given as a gift when we accept Christ as our "Blessed Hope" (Titus 2:13). That grace-gifting in turn releases the empowering presence of God into our lives in order to be who He created us to be (ambassadors for Christ), so that we can do what He calls us to do (serve as ministers of reconciliation).

Serving in the ministry of reconciliation and as ambassadors for Christ provides us with direct access to God's throne of grace. It is there that we receive ongoing/eternal grace, not only for our own needs, but also in order to gather it up and impart it to others in need—as their need(s) arise.

The context of the kingdom of God serves as a container for our citizenship, our ministry of reconciliation, our ambassadorship for Christ, and our ability to function as channels of grace to all of humankind in need of kingdom life.

APPROPRIATING GRACE (Apostolically Speaking)

Here is a brief narrative from two New Testament authors who speak to us regarding the appropriation of grace for ourselves, and the impartation of grace to others.

In 1 Cor. 1:3, 4 *(Addition mine)*, Paul says,

"Grace to you and peach from God our Father and the Lord Christ Jesus. I thank my God always concerning you for the grace of God which was given you (past tense) *in Christ Jesus."*

In that passage he is extending grace (v.3) as well as acknowledging grace already received (v.4). His personal offer of grace cannot be addressing the grace given us by God, since that's a free gift imparted to those who are redeemed in and through Christ Jesus.

"For by grace you have been saved through faith; and that not of yourselves, it is a gift of God."

~Eph. 2:8

That God given gift is what is commonly referred to in theological terms as the so-called "first work of grace." If Paul is extending grace in the manner which he appears to be, it has to be some other aspect of grace itself, since God's gift of grace is not something Paul could impart. Saving grace, redemptive grace, comes freely from the Father, our Sovereign Creator.

Therefore, what Paul is offering to others is another type of grace altogether. It is (in Wayne-Speak) appropriated grace, which is the so-called "second work of grace." It's the grace that comes after conversion.

I believe what he is imparting is the very thing that the writer of Hebrews is addressing in Heb. 4:16, which says'

"...let us draw near with confidence to the throne of grace, so that we may receive mercy and find grace to help in time of need."

Look again at the 1 Cor. 1:3, 4 passage. Notice that Paul is personally acknowledging that the first offer of grace has been given to those who are in Christ. Being "in Christ" can only take place as it relates directly to salvation. It is a gift which can only be received in one way—as part of a redemptive encounter. Paul is first giving thanks to God for giving His children grace (v.3). He's doing so (in context) after he has extended a portion of grace which is "other" than what has been received from the Father. In order to do that, he had to secure grace which he could then in turn pass on to others. That, dear reader, is exactly what Heb. 4:11 is telling us to do. I'll say it this way: Saving faith, is directly linked to saving grace. And the hope we are called to steward in our lives flows directly from the throne of grace itself—thereby creating what I call the Cycle of Hope.

"For the grace of God has appeared (past tense), *bringing salvation to all men* (see 2 Cor. 5:18-21), *instructing us to deny ungodliness and worldly desire, and to live sensibly, righteously and godly in the present age, looking for the blessed hope and the appearing of the glory of our great God and Savior, Christ Jesus."*
~Titus 2:11-13 (Addition mine)

First and foremost, we are to secure daily grace for ourselves, by approaching the throne of grace. Thereafter, in the same moment of transaction, we can request/secure grace for others in order to be able to offer it to them in their time(s) of need.

Peter echoes the same concept and intent when he says,

"…according to the foreknowledge of God the Father, by the sanctifying work of the Spirit, to obey Jesus Christ and be sprinkled with His blood: May grace and peace be yours in the fullest measure."
~1 Peter 1:2

Once again, Peters can only offer the grace he has acquired to give away, based on the portion he has received to extend. He cannot give to others that which the Father has already given to those who are "sprinkled with His blood." However, he can (and we should) draw upon and drink deeply from its every-flowing fountain.

"As each one has received a special gift, employ it in serving one another as good stewards of the *manifold (Multi-faceted) grace of God."
~1 Peter 4:19 (Addition mine)

Simply stated: We are to first receive the gift of grace through salvation. Then, we are to employ it in serving one another through our good stewardship of the grace we are continually given as we appropriate it.

The direct acquisition and extension of grace from God's throne of grace, into our lives, and then on to others in their particular time(s) of need, is the protocol and process which we as followers of Christ should be taking part in on a regular, ongoing, daily basis. That's how we become channels, or channelers, of grace. May the Holy Ghost grant you knowledge, understanding, and wisdom as you work through what I've just presented.

Knowledge is Information
Understanding is Interpretation
Wisdom is Application

A Promise

"For the earth will be filled with the knowledge of the glory of the Lord, As the waters cover the sea."
~Hab. 2:14

A Prayer

"Thy kingdom come, Thy will be done, in earth as it is in heaven."
~Mt. 6:10 - KJV

Author's Prayer

My prayer for you regarding the impact of this entire

narrative is that it will stir you to consider each and every aspect of your kingdom citizenship deeply and often take your job assignment as a minister of reconciliation seriously.

Steward your job title as an ambassador for Christ as the treasured gift that it is.

Open yourself up to living as a channel of grace for anyone and everyone who needs it.

"Acquire wisdom. Acquire understanding. Do not forget."
~Pro. 4:5

EPILOGUE

There are two ways to see life here on earth:

1. A world-view is a way of seeing life on earth from a temporal vantage point. It is based on morals, ethics, and culturally-formulated aspects.
2. A biblical world-view is a way of seeing life based on the Word of God, Holy Rite, the Bible.

One will last until we die. The other will endure eternally. One is common to humankind. The other is uncommon—it was supernaturally created and sustained. One is popular among many. One is practiced by a few. I'll just leave this here.

VISION

I have a vision, of a world yet to come
Where only peace, and sweet release
Flow from the Master's throne

I have a vision, of the kingdom from above
Coming down in light, making all things bright
And bathing the world in love

It's for you to share, it's for those who dare
To believe what they cannot see
There's a choice to make, there's a path to take
That leads from here to eternity

I have a vision, there are some who share this dream
As "The Day" draws near, we prepare to hear
The sound of the trumpets ring
At that call, we'll all bow and sing
Proclaiming Jesus Christ as King

(W. Berry / See & Say Songs, BMI)

If you're interested
PREVIOUS PROJECTS
(From back in the daze)

The link below will get you to all of my on line recorded audio & video products from back in the daze. Along with that, you'll also find a few songs of mine recorded by other artists.

All sales from Amazon and CD Baby projects go directly toward funding mission sojourning on the African continent through OUTBOUND MINISTRIES INTERNATIONAL.

For more information visit:

https://www.facebook.com/seeandsaysongs

Also Available From
WordCrafts Press

Pondering(s)
   by Wayne Berry

Pressing Foward
   by April Poynter

Morning Mist: Stories from the Water's Edge
   by Barbie Loflin

Youth Ministry is Easy! and 9 other lies
   by Aaron Shaver

Illuminations
   by Paula K. Parker & Tracy Sugg

A Scarlet Cord of Hope
   by Sheryl Griffin

www.wordcrafts.net

www.ingramcontent.com/pod-product-compliance
Lightning Source LLC
Chambersburg PA
CBHW052139110526
44591CB00012B/1790